SMART SKETCH BOOK 3

Oogie Art's step-by-step guide to drawing still life objects with charcoal and soft pastels.

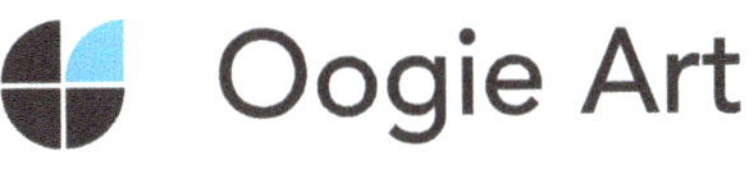

Oogie Art's SmartSketchbook™
An Expert's Guide to Still Life in Charcoal and Pastel
First Edition, Copyright © 2015

Produced and Edited by
Oogie Art
New York, NY

© Text
Oogie Art

© Photographs
Licensed under Oogie Art®

Directed by
Wook Choi

Assistant Directed by
Clara Lu

Drawings by
Jee Hwang

Tips by
Wook Choi

Published and Distributed by
Oogie Publishing House
New York, NY
www.oogiepublishinghouse.com
(212) 714-1011

ISBN 978-0-9855809-4-0
Printed in the United States

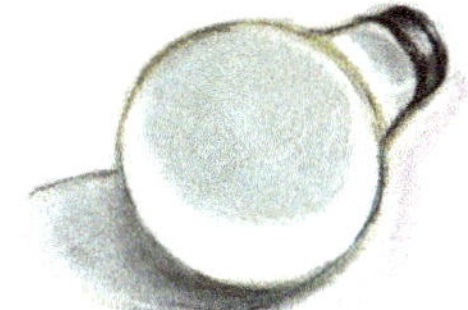
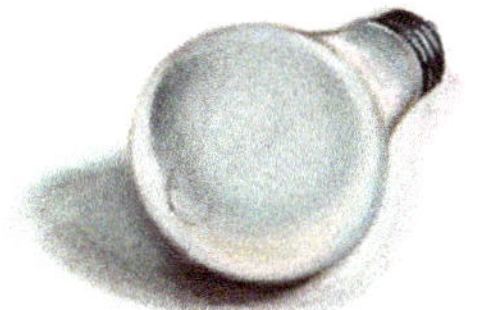
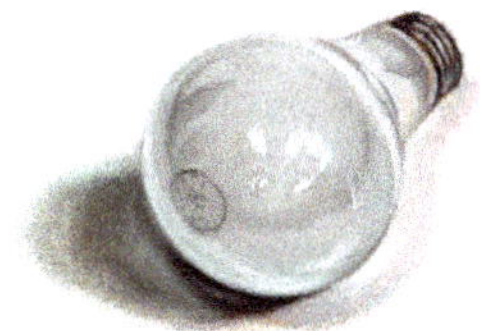

CONTENTS

Introduction to Soft Pastels

Soft Pastels make an excellent introduction to color. As a dry and soft drawing tool, pastels handle similarly to vine charcoal, are easy to blend, and have sets that come in a full spectrum of colors to choose from. Unlike paints, pastel colors must be mixed and layered on the paper, so a wide range of colors is recommended.

While pastels crumble easily their colors do not fade, crack or yellow over time.

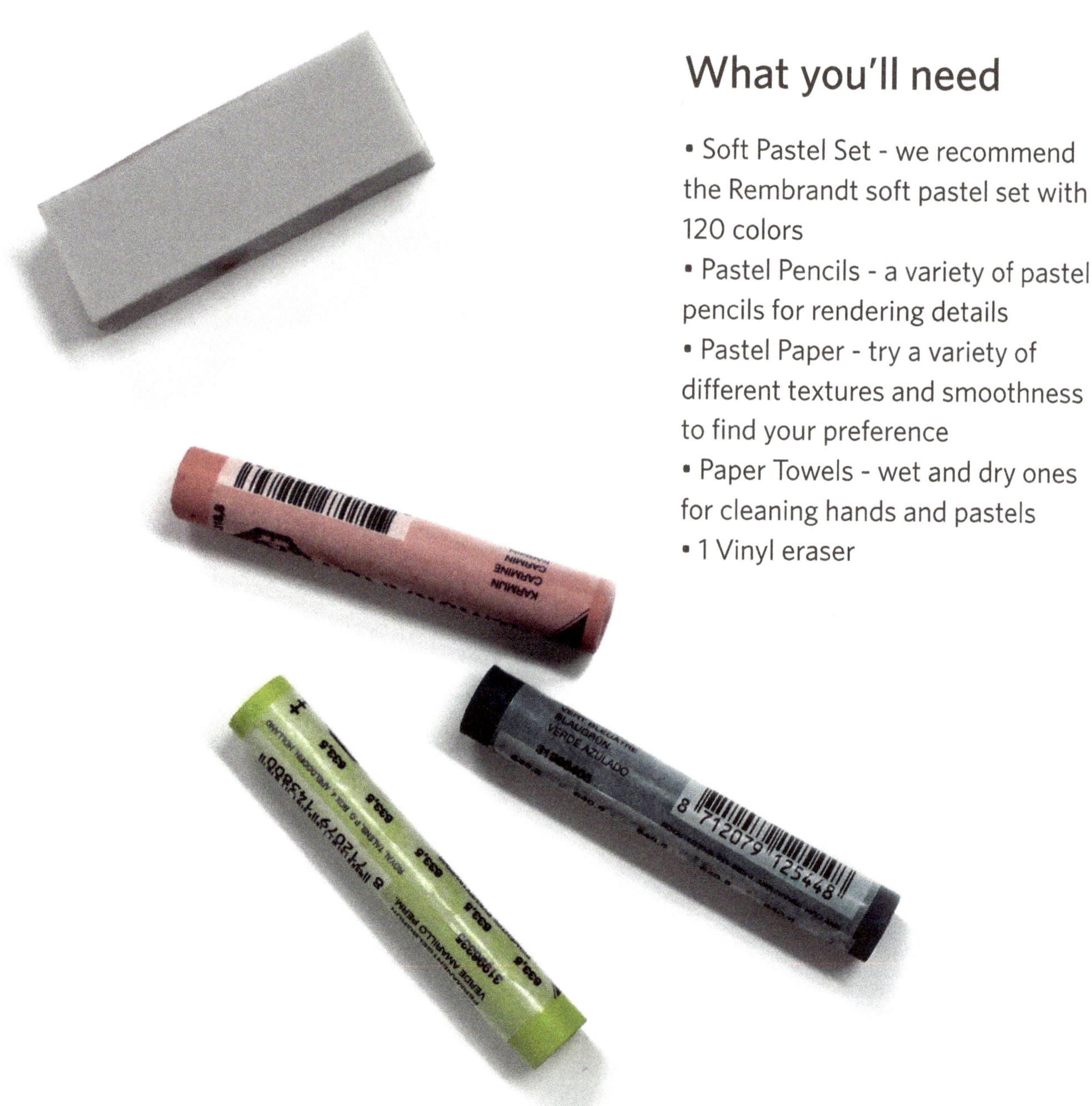

What you'll need

- Soft Pastel Set - we recommend the Rembrandt soft pastel set with 120 colors
- Pastel Pencils - a variety of pastel pencils for rendering details
- Pastel Paper - try a variety of different textures and smoothness to find your preference
- Paper Towels - wet and dry ones for cleaning hands and pastels
- 1 Vinyl eraser

Forms and Types of Soft Pastels

There are two general types of soft pastels, stick and pencil. Sticks are more suitable for larger areas or softer surfaces, while pencils are perfect for creating controlled, detailed marks. There are many more differences between types of medium and level of density.
Refer to the chart below for more details.

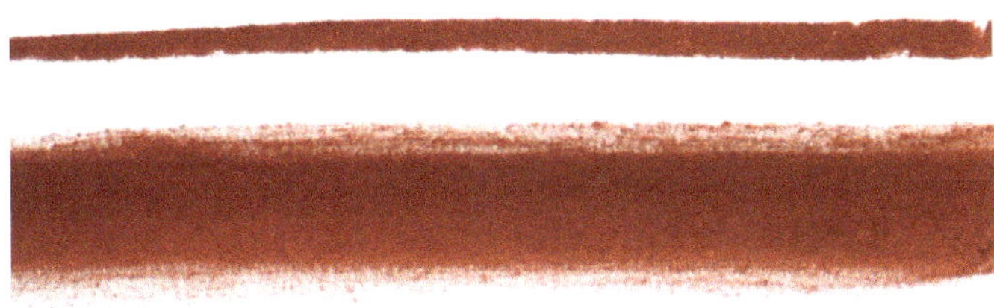

Extra Soft Pastel

Typically used to start a drawing because of its rich tones and hues; best for creating the under layer of a drawing before using soft pastels.

Soft Pastel

Most commonly used form of pastel due to its high concentration of pigmentation and slightly more compressed nature. More suitable for wide areas or softer surfaces. Also great for expressing light when used with a slightly wet brush.

Pastel Pencil

Suitable for creating controlled marks and details.

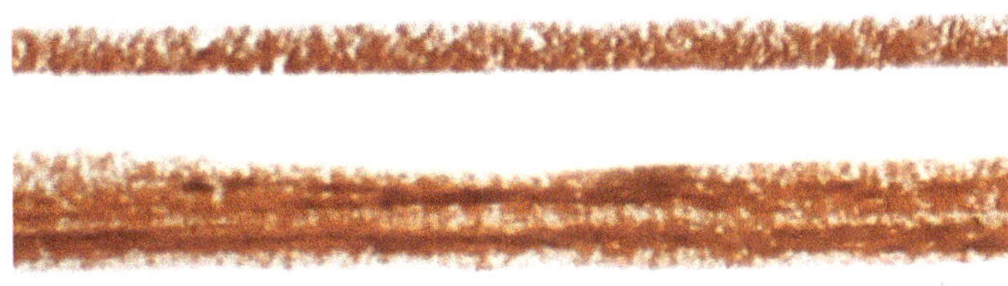

Oil Pastel

Much softer and has a higher concentration of pigment compared to crayons. Due to its intensity of color, it is great for expressing rough texture. It can be used to cover up lighter areas with dark colors. It is bound with wax and oil, can be spread like oil paint to create strong, buttery strokes. Using turpentine gives it a lightly colored effect.

Pastel Techniques

Line - The simplest way of using pastel is through line. This is a great way of showing expression and gesture. The harder you press, the thicker the line. For thinner lines, press lightly or use a sharp edge. Use your whole arm to create a more gestural and expressive line. This is useful for blocking in your drawing before adding details.

For hard lines, shapes, and textures, a hard pastel may also be used.

There are a number of techniques to correct any pastel mistakes. If the pigment hasn't been applied too heavily, a kneaded eraser can be used to help lift off some color. However this can damage the surface of the drawing.

Pastels should be handled with care since they are easily smudged. Use a spray-on sealant or fixative to set your work and prevent smearing.

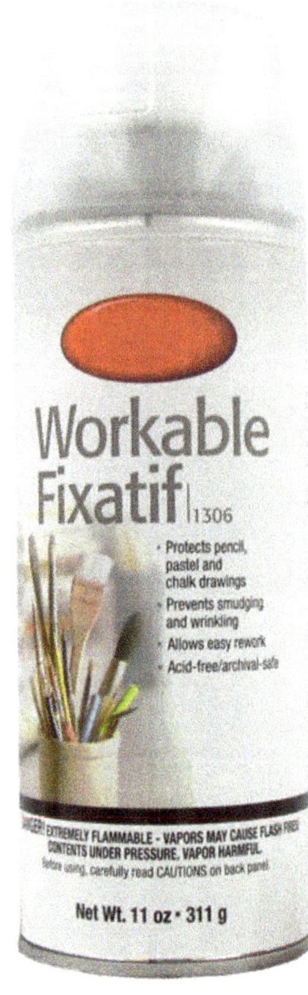

Color Mixing Techniques

Pastels can be used for various types of interpretation. Try the exercises below to practice different types of marks.

1. Use the entire side length of the pastel stick to quickly fill in large areas of color.

2. Pastels are versatile enough to create controlled, fine works of art. Sharpen the edge of the stick to create basic outlines of shapes and fine lines.

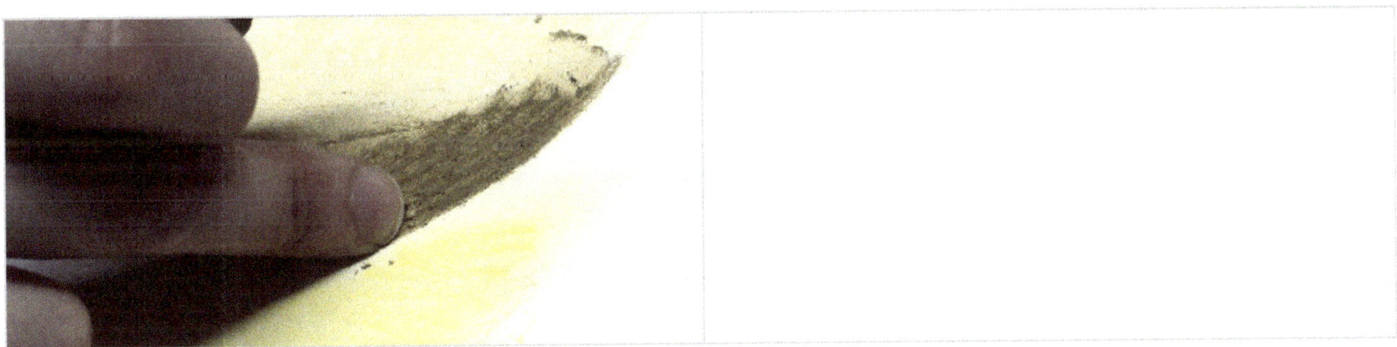

3. Using the short edge on the ends of a pastel stick, create thin, even lines for linear textures in sketching.

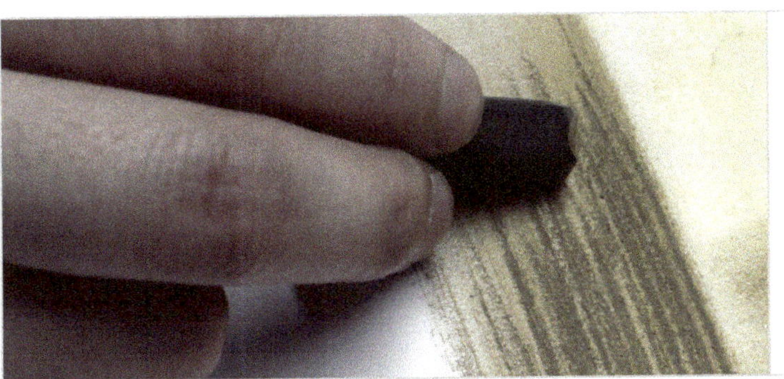

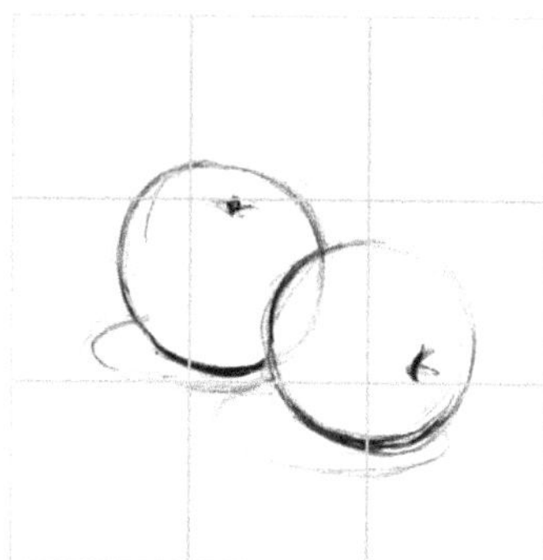

Using vine charcoal, sketch the general shape of the apples. Draw the entire apple even if it is covered by the other, to get a full sense of the shape.

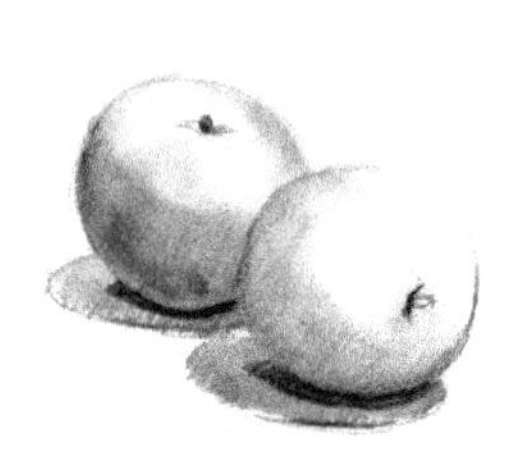

Identify the direction of the light source and shade in the general areas of shadow using vine charcoal and smudging with your fingers.

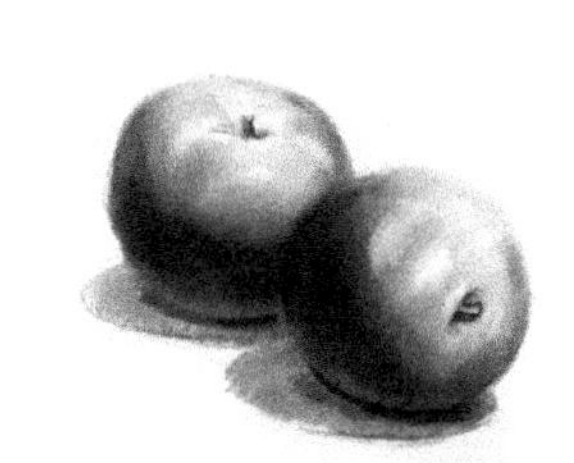

Continue to identify the darks, lights, and middle tones using a combination of vine and compressed charcoal.

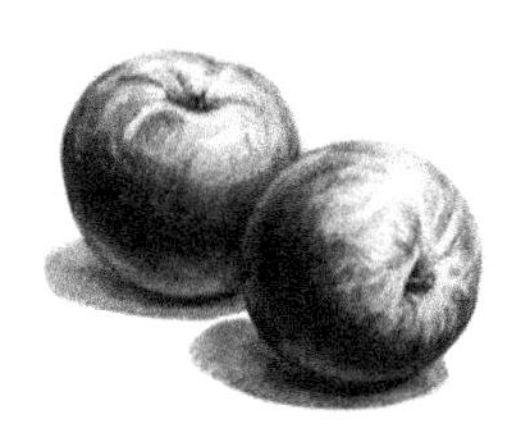

Make sure to use the entire range of tones to fully develop your drawing. Only on the last step define the details, using compressed charcoal and your eraser.

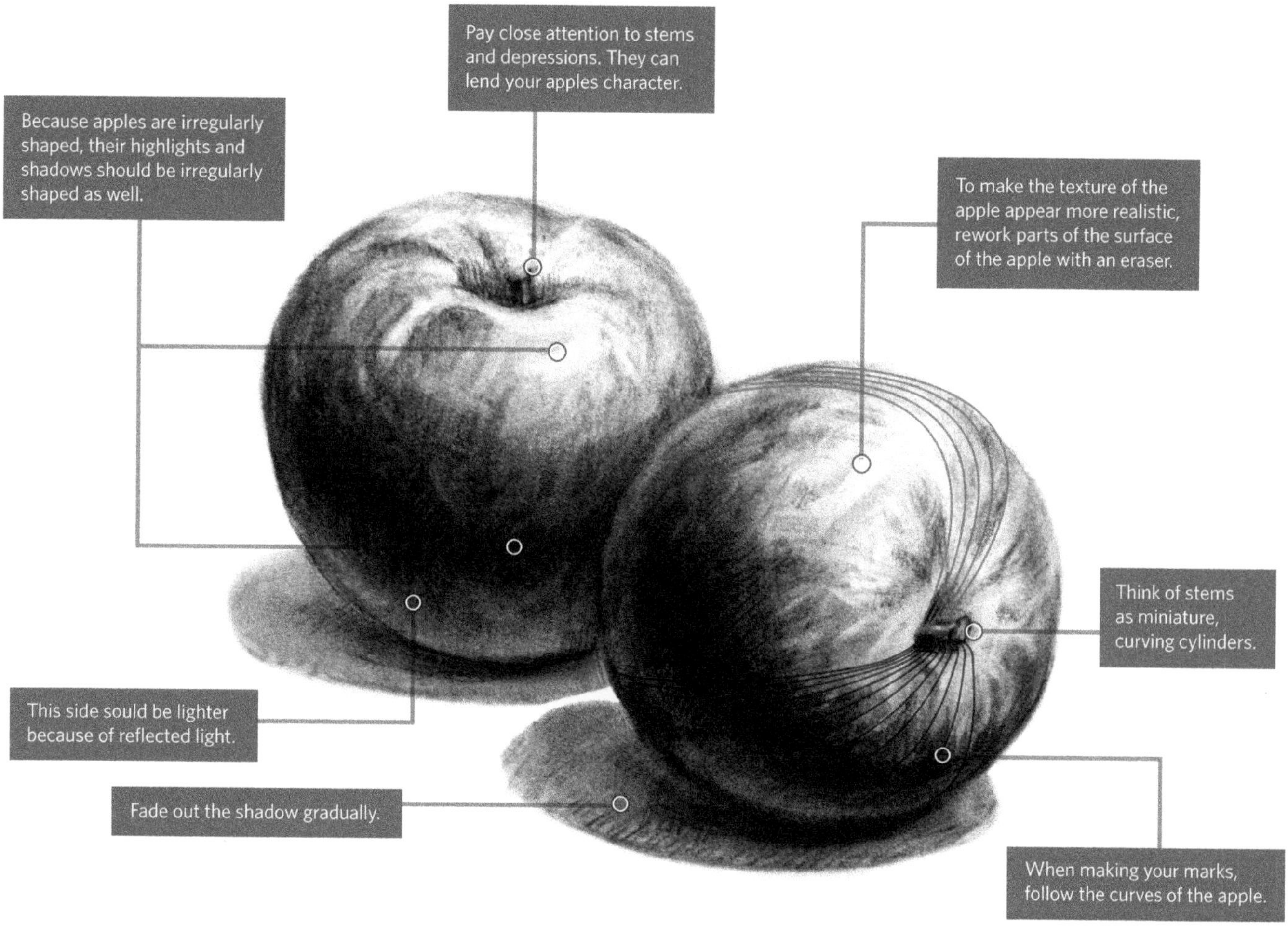

Pay close attention to stems and depressions. They can lend your apples character.

Because apples are irregularly shaped, their highlights and shadows should be irregularly shaped as well.

To make the texture of the apple appear more realistic, rework parts of the surface of the apple with an eraser.

Think of stems as miniature, curving cylinders.

This side sould be lighter because of reflected light.

Fade out the shadow gradually.

When making your marks, follow the curves of the apple.

Now try drawing the apple yourself.

Now that you have practiced how to draw an apple still life in charcoal following a step-by-step tutorial, use the page on the right to try and draw from life. You can draw from the picture below or set up your own still life and try different variations of still life compositions.

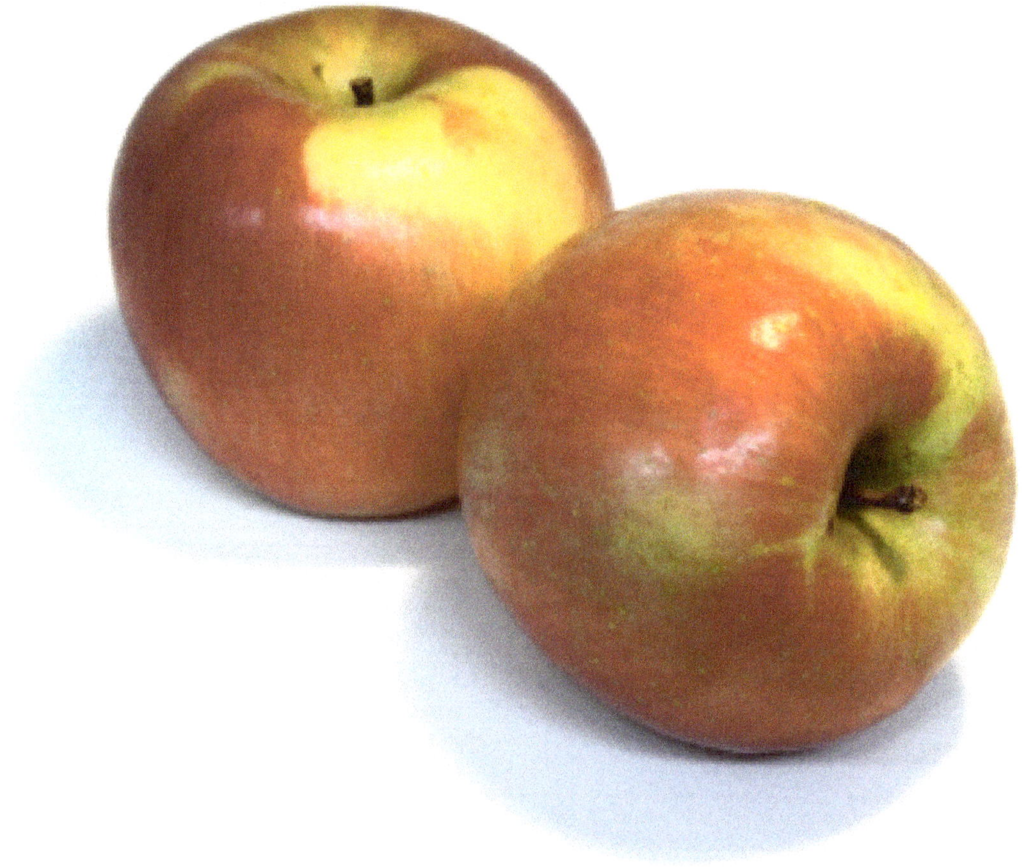

Now try drawing the apple using the reference picture without any grid lines.

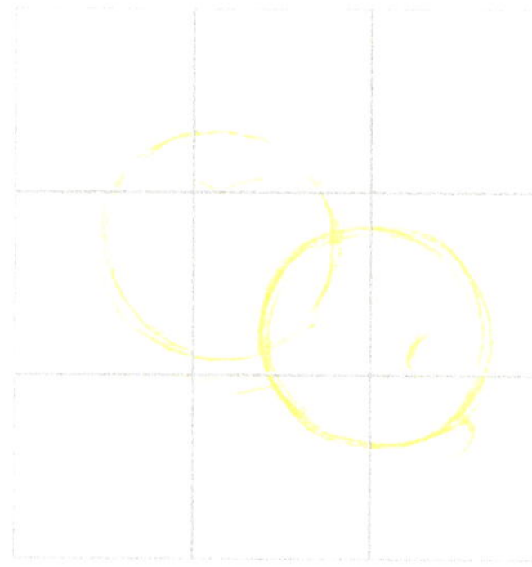

Using a yellow cadmium pastel, sketch the general shape of the apples. Draw the entire apple even if it is covered by the other, to get a full sense of the shape.

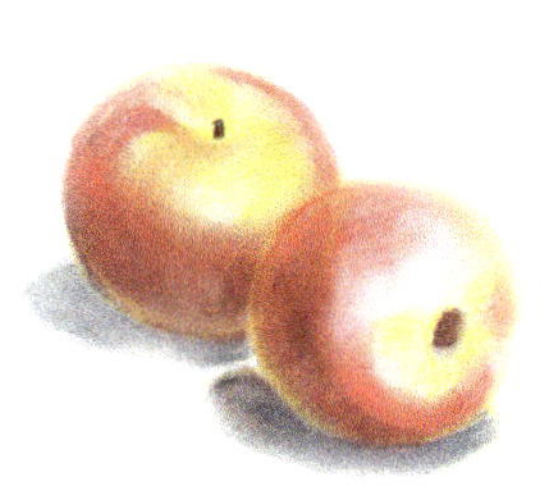

Start to incorporate color and volume using a red color and smudging with your fingers. Notice that it's not a flat shade of red all over, but lighter and darker in some areas. Use a bluish-gray for the shadow.

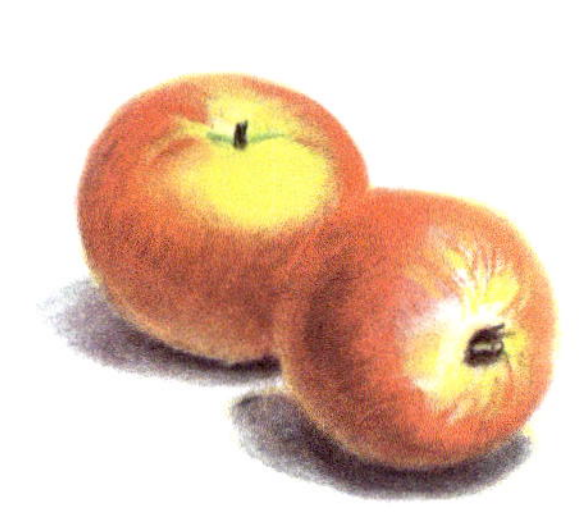

Continue to use reds, yellows, and oranges to define the areas of lights and darks. Use a dark umber for the dark areas of shadow.

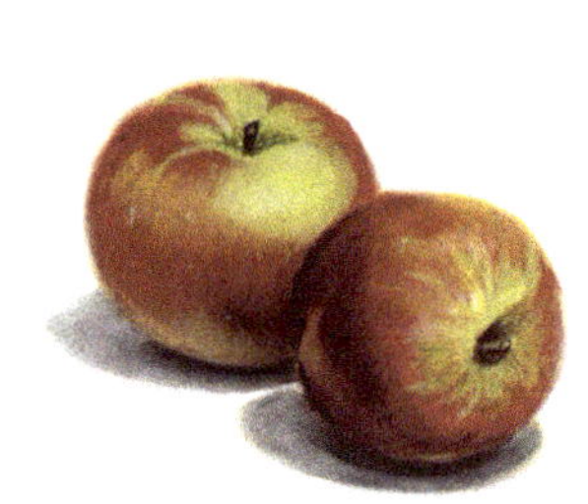

Make sure to use a full range of warm tones to fully express the volume of the apples. Use cooler yellows, reds and greens for the reflected areas and stems. Save the small shadow and highlight details for the last.

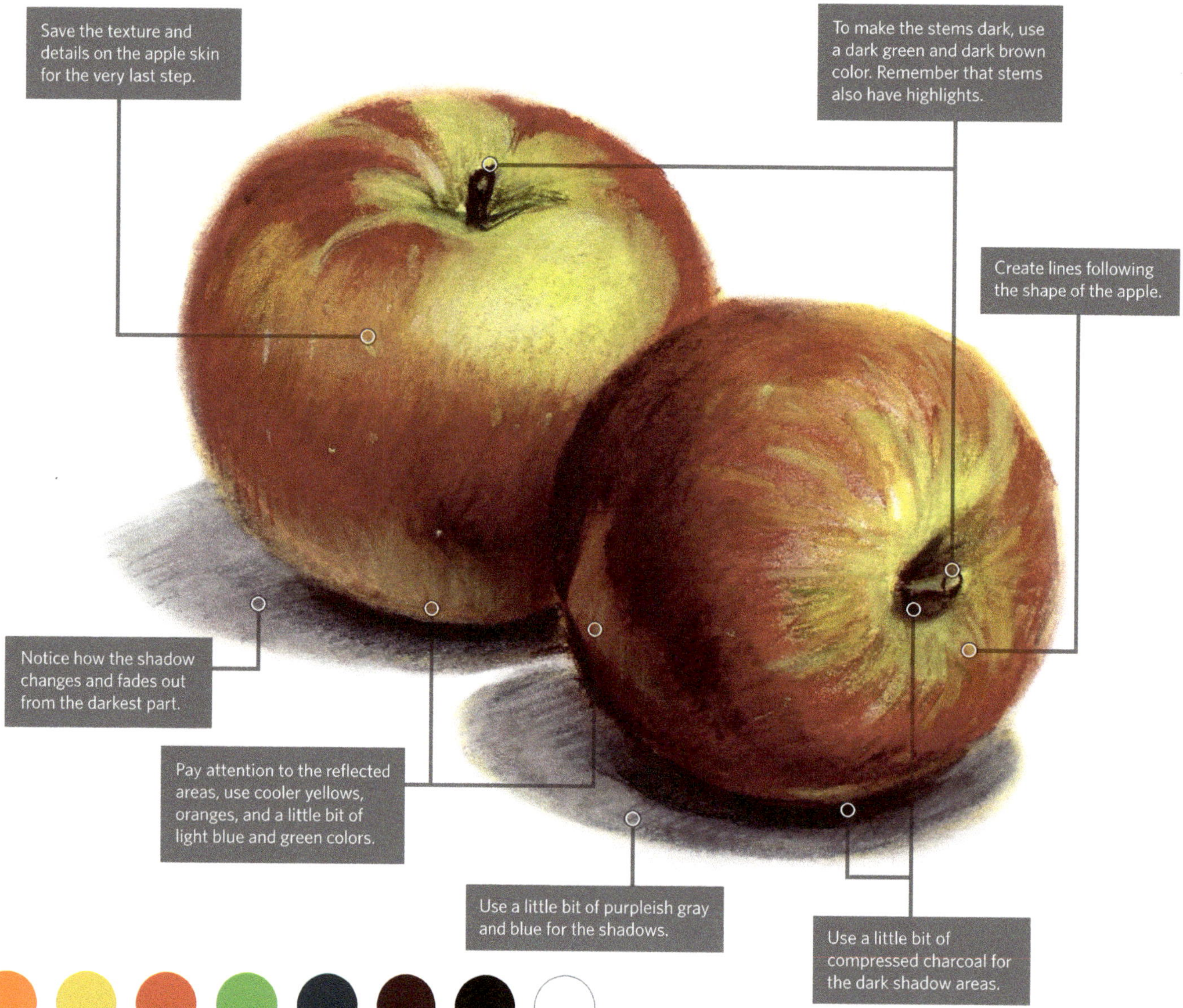

Save the texture and details on the apple skin for the very last step.

To make the stems dark, use a dark green and dark brown color. Remember that stems also have highlights.

Create lines following the shape of the apple.

Notice how the shadow changes and fades out from the darkest part.

Pay attention to the reflected areas, use cooler yellows, oranges, and a little bit of light blue and green colors.

Use a little bit of purpleish gray and blue for the shadows.

Use a little bit of compressed charcoal for the dark shadow areas.

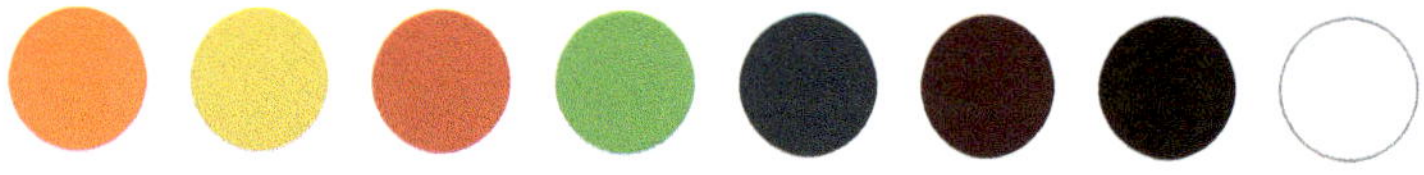

cadmium orange · cadmium yellow · cadmium red · light green · viridian · burnt umber · charcoal · white

Now try drawing the apple yourself.

Now that you have practiced how to draw an apple still life in pastel following a step-by-step tutorial, use the page on the right to try and draw from life. You can draw from the picture below or set up your own still life and try different variations of still life compositions.

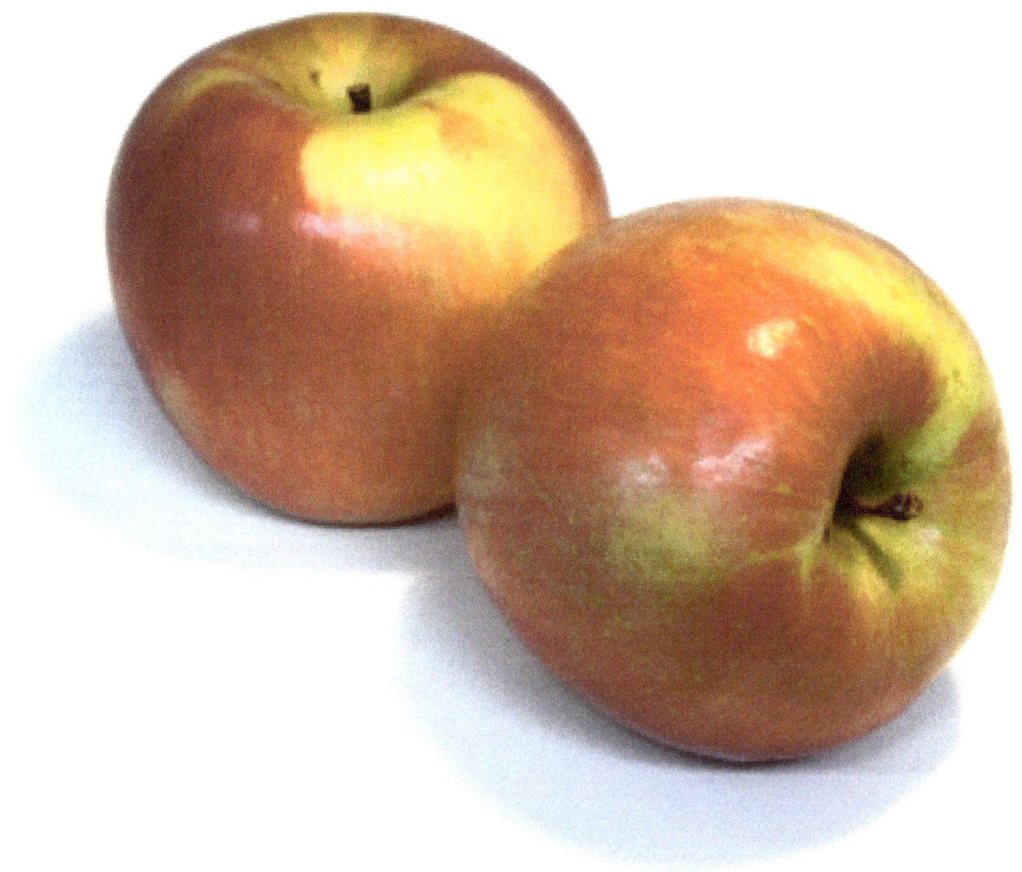

Now try drawing the apple using the reference picture without any grid lines.

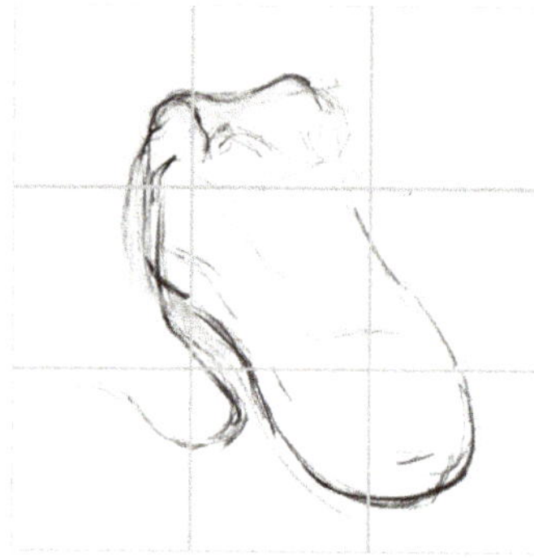

Using vine charcoal, sketch the general geometric shape of the shoe with a center line through the middle to identify the major planes of the shoe.

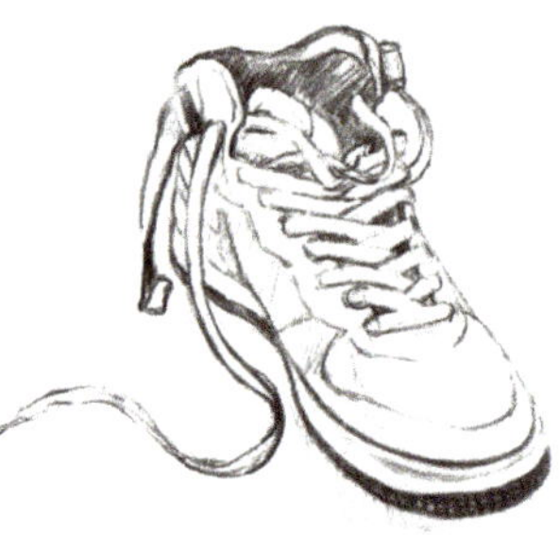

Identify general details, then identify the direction of the light source and shade in the general areas of shadow using vine charcoal.

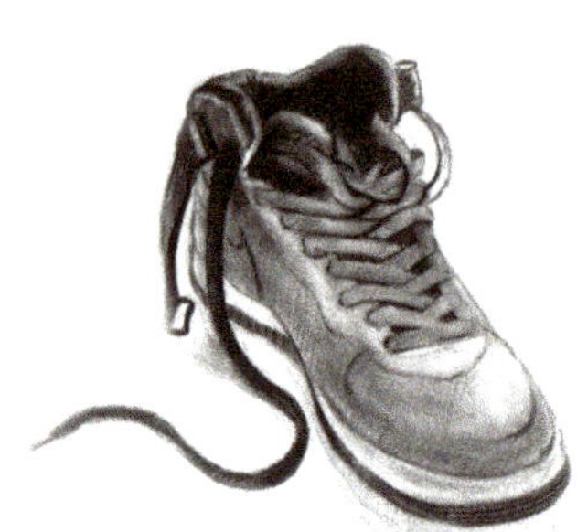

Continue to identify the darks, lights, and middle tones using a combination of vine and compressed charcoal while smudging areas of general shadow.

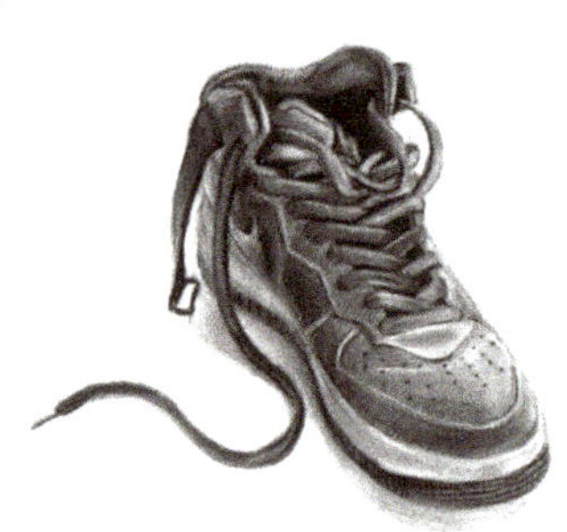

Make sure to use the entire range of tones to fully develop your drawing. Only on the last step define the details in the stitching and holes of the shoe.

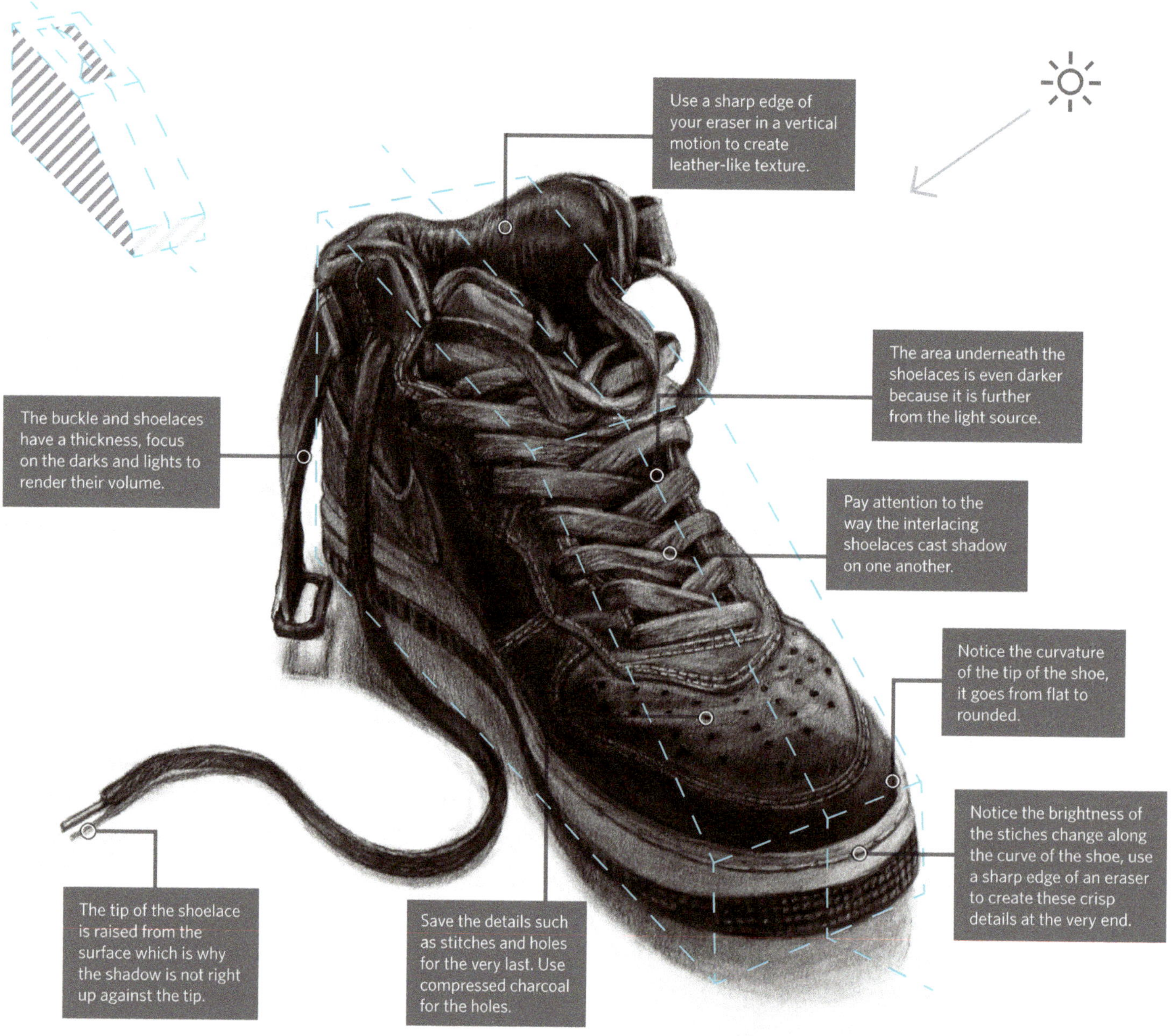

Use a sharp edge of your eraser in a vertical motion to create leather-like texture.

The buckle and shoelaces have a thickness, focus on the darks and lights to render their volume.

The area underneath the shoelaces is even darker because it is further from the light source.

Pay attention to the way the interlacing shoelaces cast shadow on one another.

Notice the curvature of the tip of the shoe, it goes from flat to rounded.

Notice the brightness of the stiches change along the curve of the shoe, use a sharp edge of an eraser to create these crisp details at the very end.

The tip of the shoelace is raised from the surface which is why the shadow is not right up against the tip.

Save the details such as stitches and holes for the very last. Use compressed charcoal for the holes.

Now try drawing the shoe yourself.

Now that you have practiced how to draw a shoe in charcoal following a step-by-step tutorial, use the page on the right to try and draw from life. You can draw from the picture below or set up your own still life and try different variations of still life compositions.

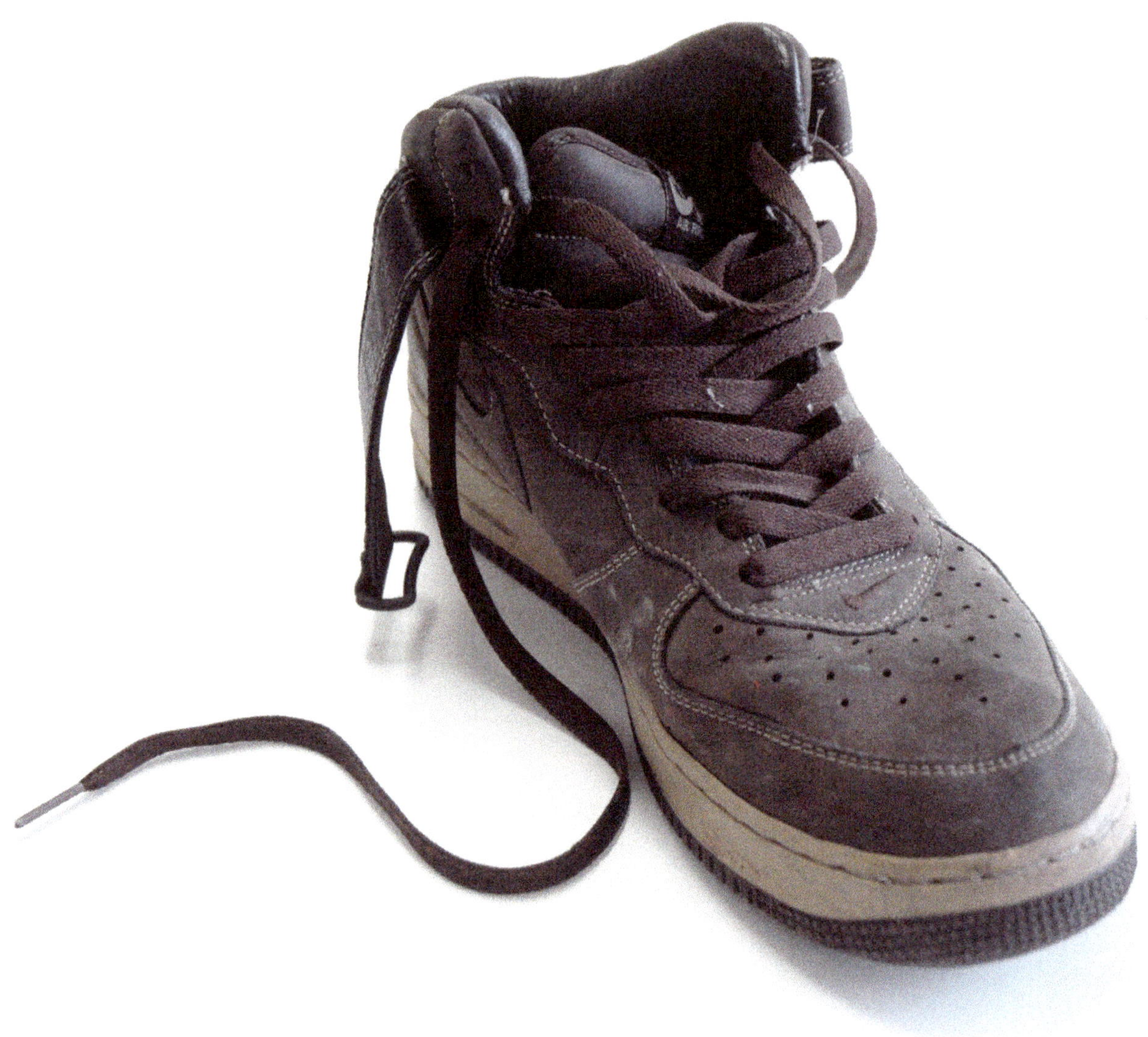

Now try drawing the shoe using the reference picture without any grid lines.

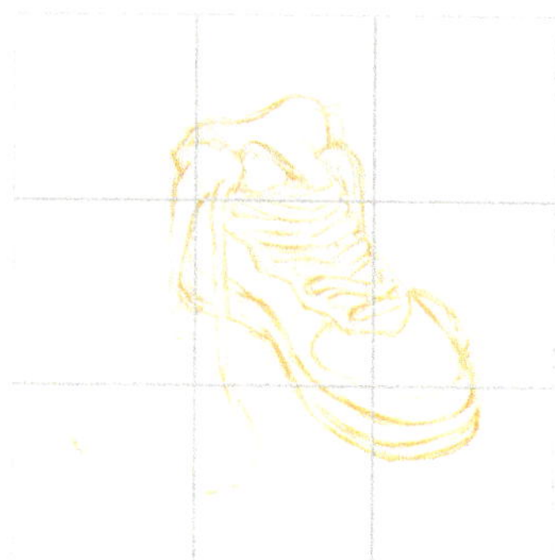

Using a light yellow ochre, sketch the general geometric shape of the shoe with a center line through the middle to identify the major planes of the shoe.

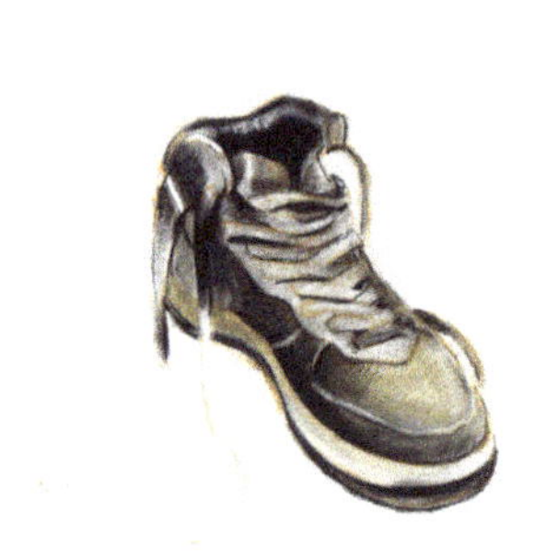

Without using white, begin shading in general areas of shadow with burnt umber and raw umber to create volume.

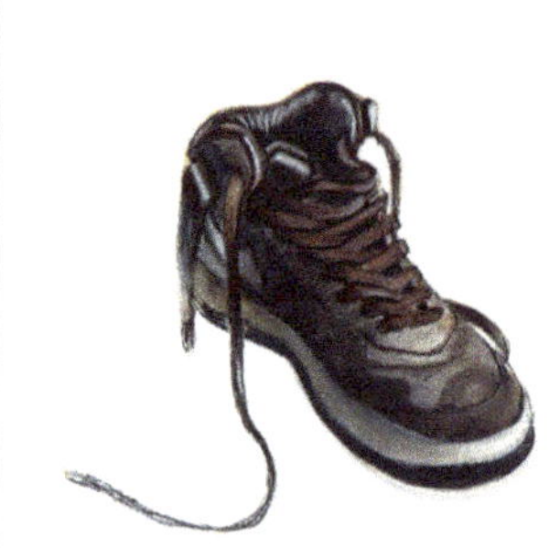

Continue to use a range of deep reds, light and dark burnt umbers, and a little bit of light bluish greens for the cool areas of shadow.

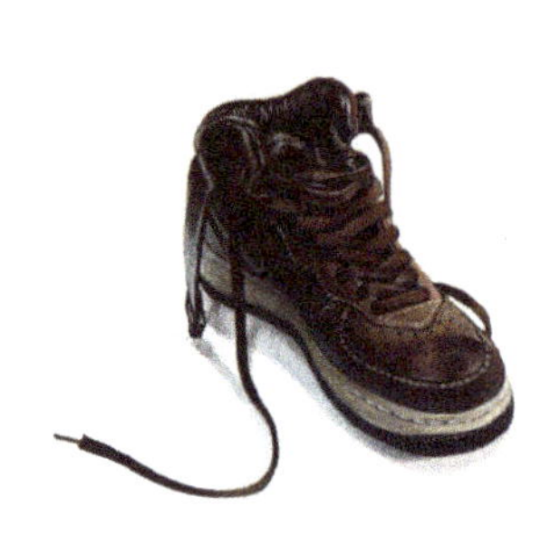

As you approach the end, use more warm tones to create more contrast from warm and cool areas, using ochres, sienna, reds, and some pinks.

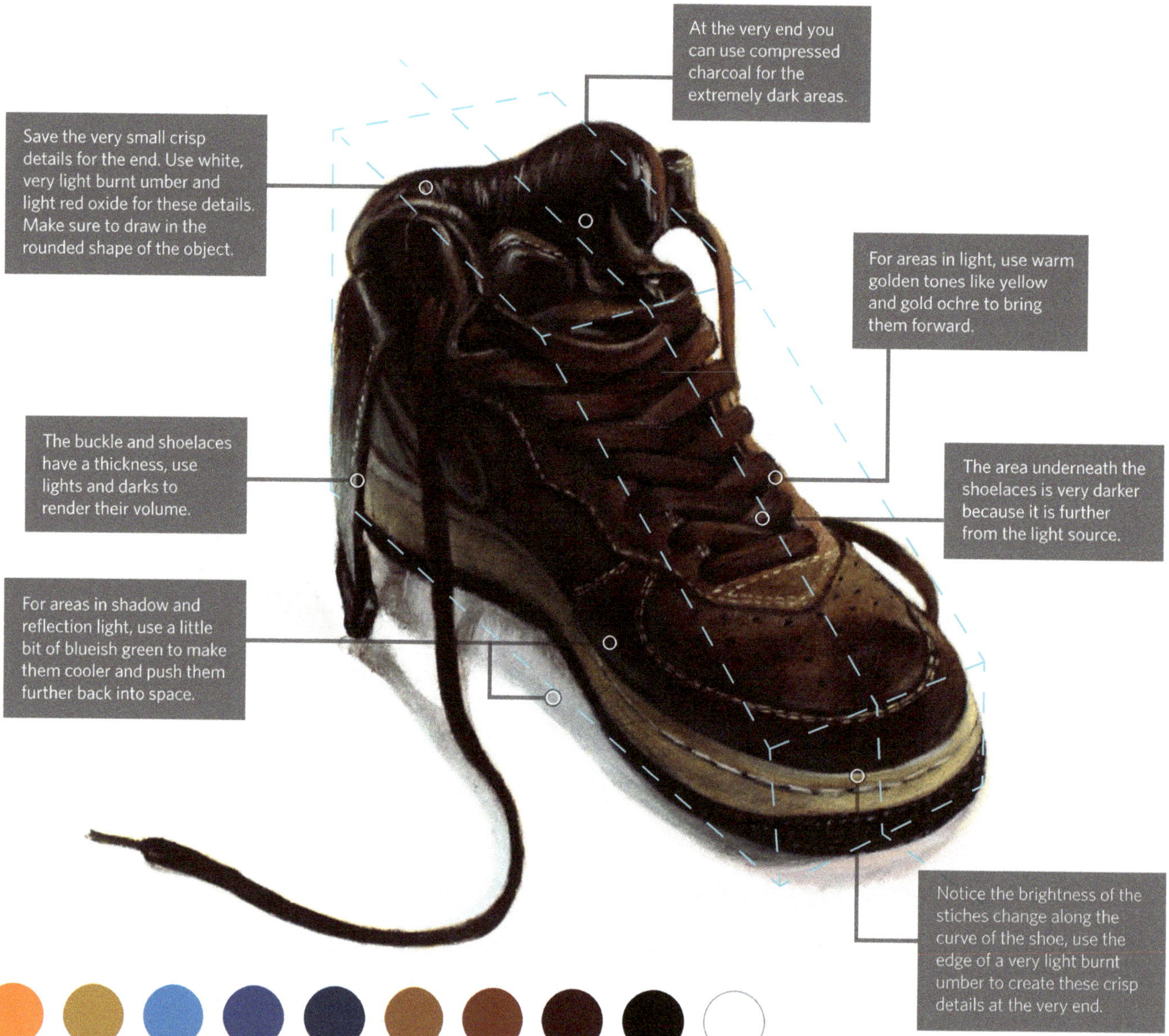

At the very end you can use compressed charcoal for the extremely dark areas.

Save the very small crisp details for the end. Use white, very light burnt umber and light red oxide for these details. Make sure to draw in the rounded shape of the object.

For areas in light, use warm golden tones like yellow and gold ochre to bring them forward.

The buckle and shoelaces have a thickness, use lights and darks to render their volume.

The area underneath the shoelaces is very darker because it is further from the light source.

For areas in shadow and reflection light, use a little bit of blueish green to make them cooler and push them further back into space.

Notice the brightness of the stiches change along the curve of the shoe, use the edge of a very light burnt umber to create these crisp details at the very end.

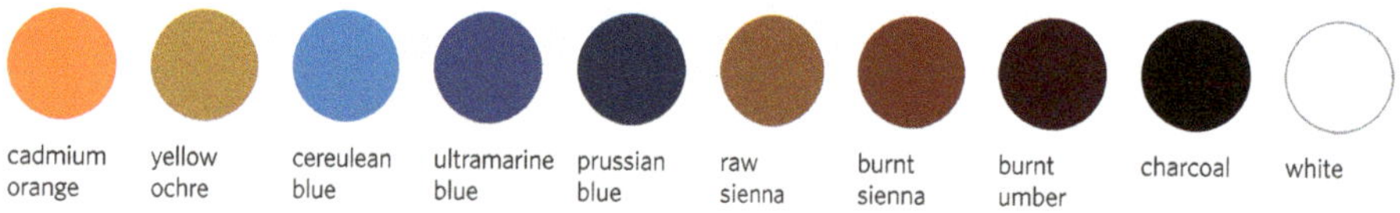

cadmium orange · yellow ochre · cereulean blue · ultramarine blue · prussian blue · raw sienna · burnt sienna · burnt umber · charcoal · white

Now try drawing the shoe yourself.

Now that you have practiced how to draw a shoe in pastel following a step-by-step tutorial, use the page on the right to try and draw from life. You can draw from the picture below or set up your own still life and try different variations of still life compositions.

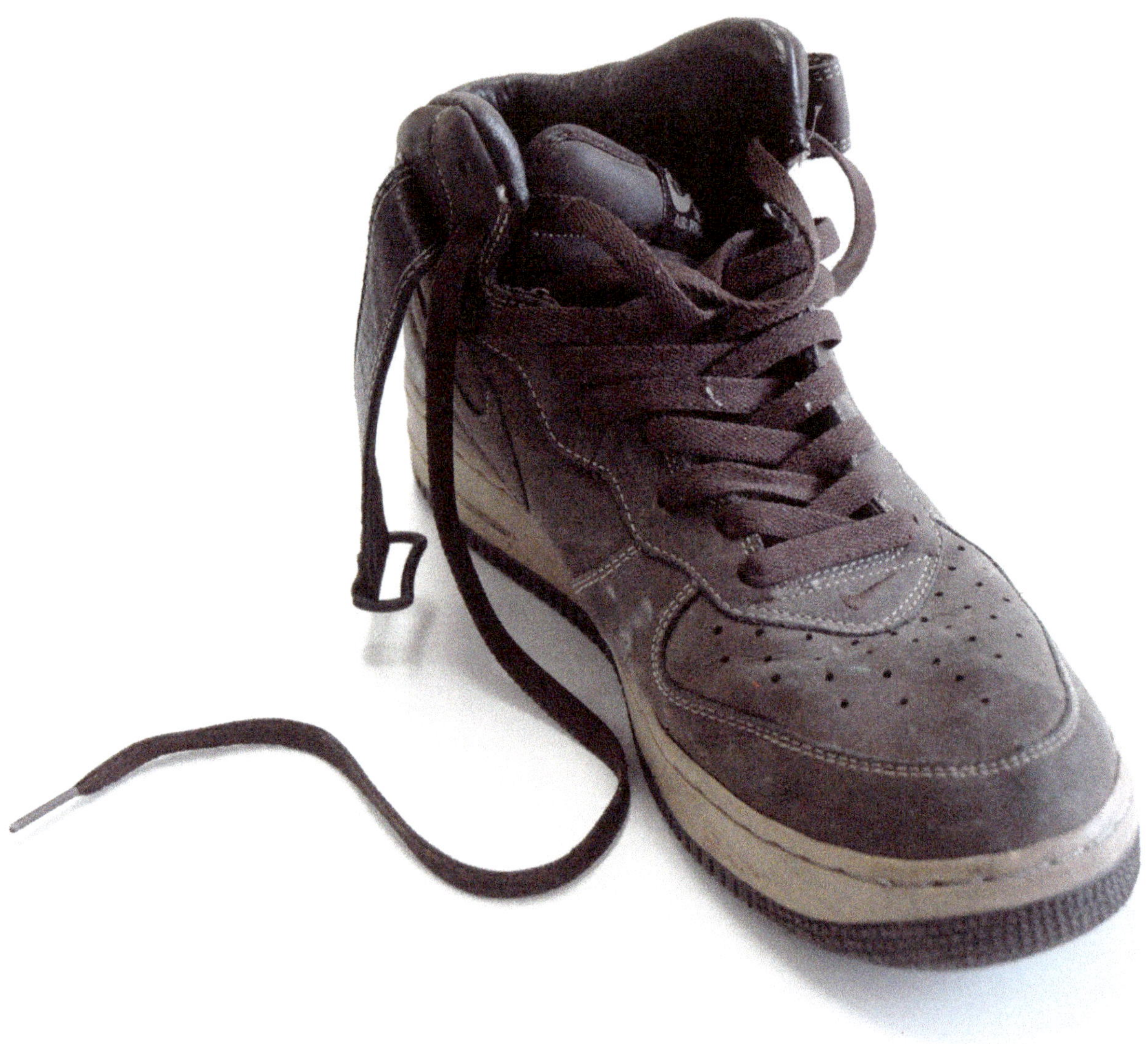

Now try drawing the shoe using the reference picture without any grid lines.

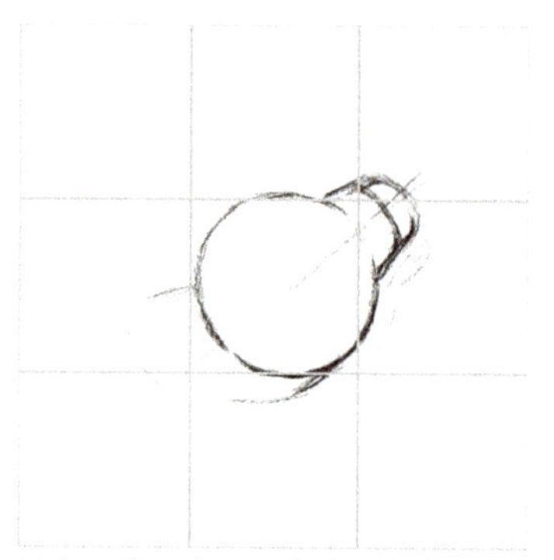

Using vine charcoal, sketch the general shape of the lightbulb. Draw a center line to imitate the lightbulb in perspective.

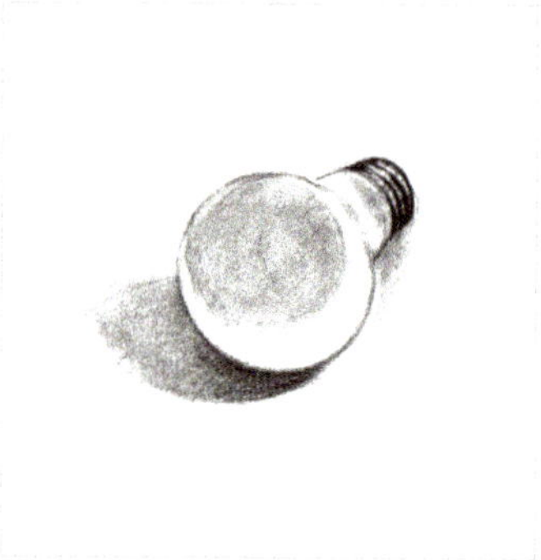

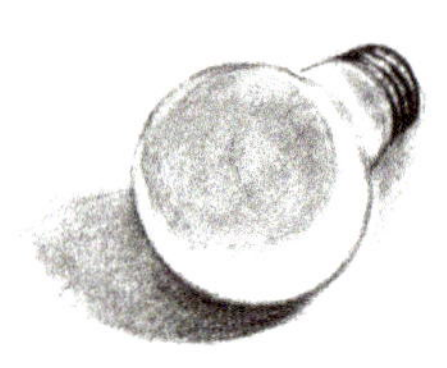

Identify the direction of the light source and shade in the general areas of shadow using vine charcoal.

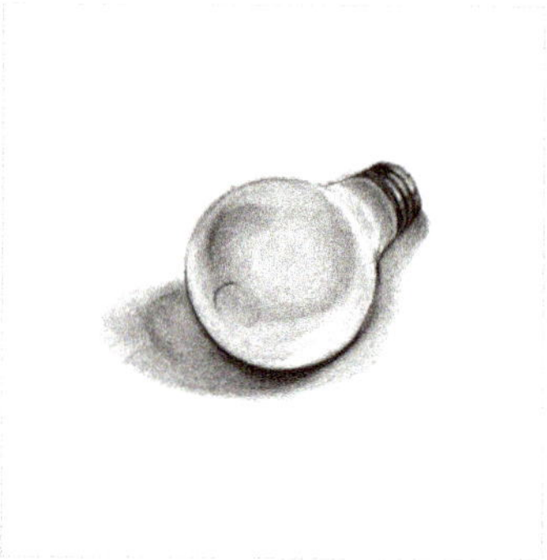

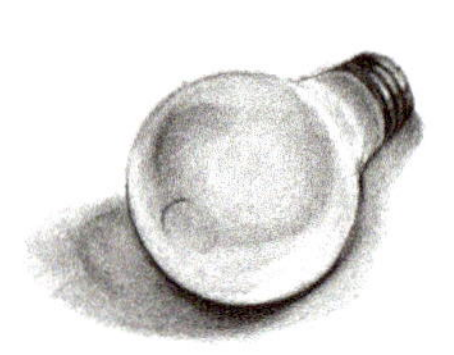

Continue to identify the darks, lights, and middle tones using a combination of vine and compressed charcoal. Make sure to blend by smudging to imitate the smooth surface of the lightbulb.

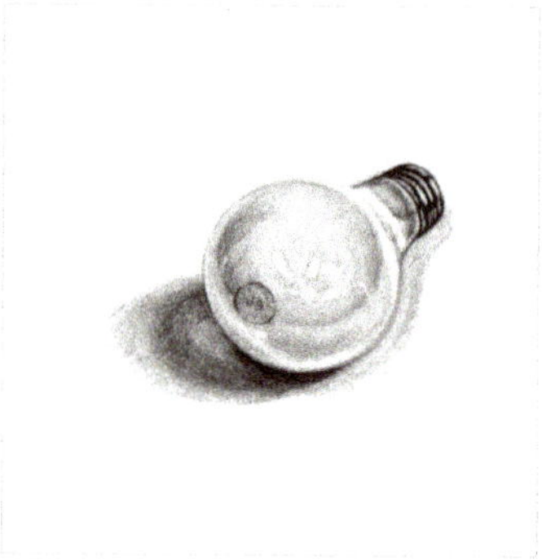

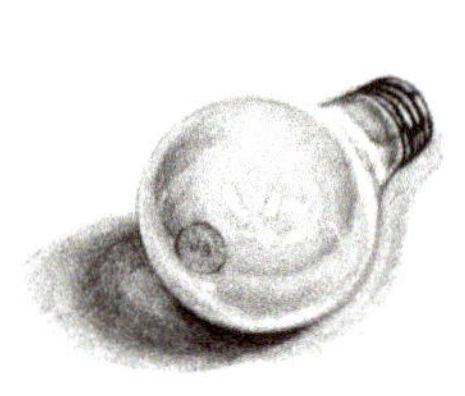

Make sure to use the entire range of tones to fully develop your drawing. Only on the last step define the details without smudging too much.

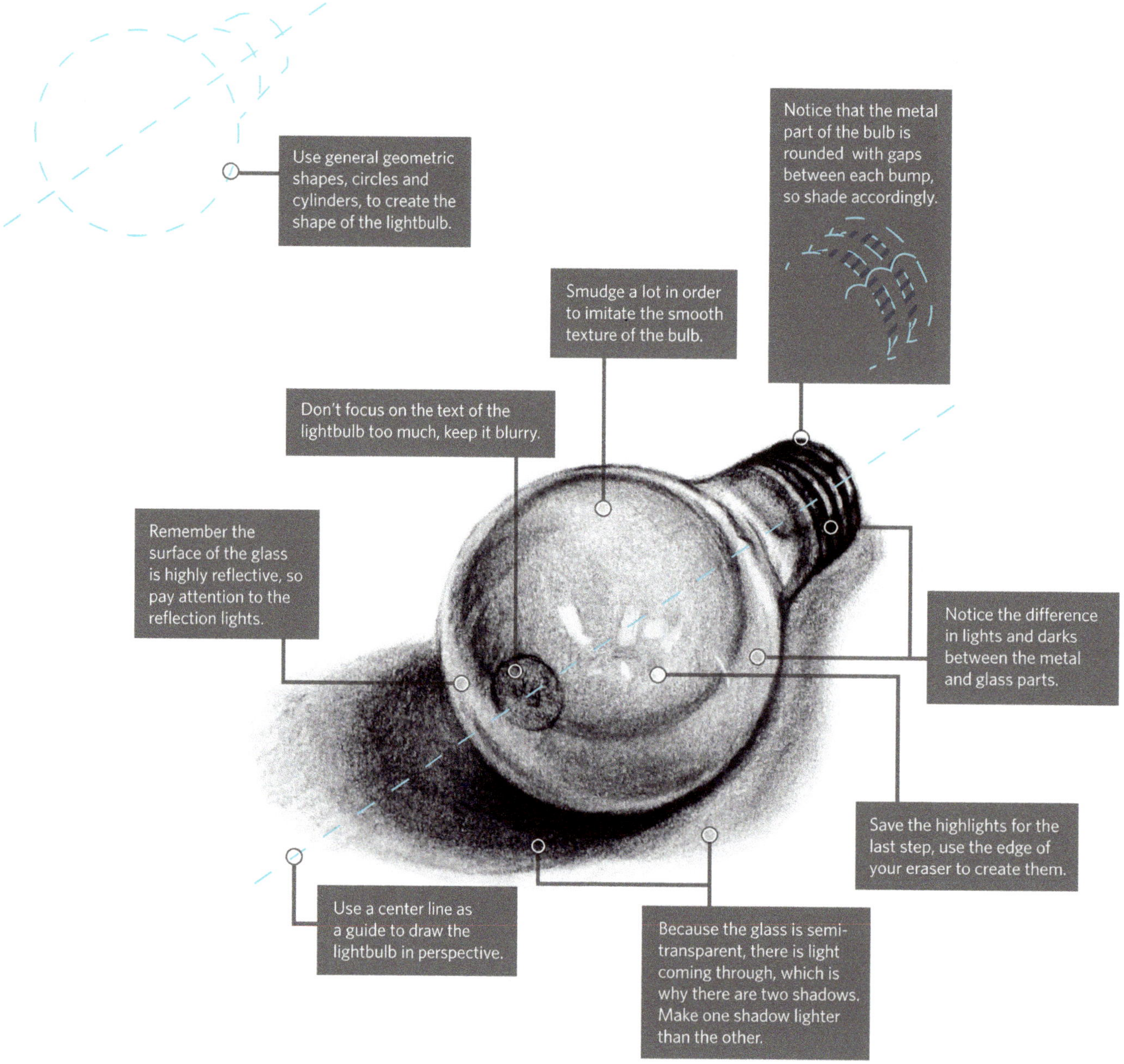

Use general geometric shapes, circles and cylinders, to create the shape of the lightbulb.

Notice that the metal part of the bulb is rounded with gaps between each bump, so shade accordingly.

Smudge a lot in order to imitate the smooth texture of the bulb.

Don't focus on the text of the lightbulb too much, keep it blurry.

Remember the surface of the glass is highly reflective, so pay attention to the reflection lights.

Notice the difference in lights and darks between the metal and glass parts.

Save the highlights for the last step, use the edge of your eraser to create them.

Use a center line as a guide to draw the lightbulb in perspective.

Because the glass is semi-transparent, there is light coming through, which is why there are two shadows. Make one shadow lighter than the other.

Now try drawing the light bulb yourself.

Now that you have practiced how to draw a lightbulb in charcoal following a step-by-step tutorial, use the page on the right to try and draw from life. You can draw from the picture below or set up your own still life and try different variations of still life compositions.

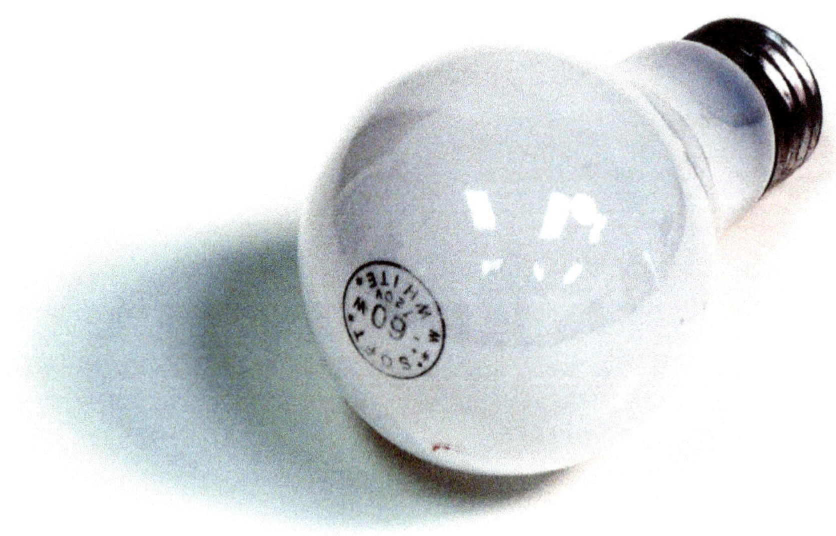

Now try drawing the light bulb using the reference picture without any grid lines.

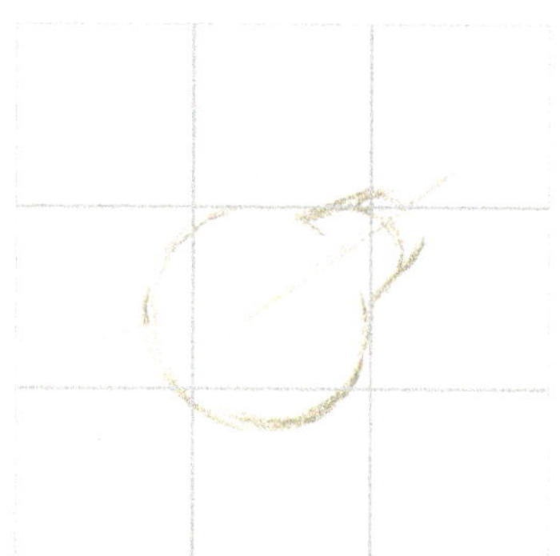

Using a gray color, sketch the general shape of the lightbulb. Draw a center line to imitate the lightbulb in perspective.

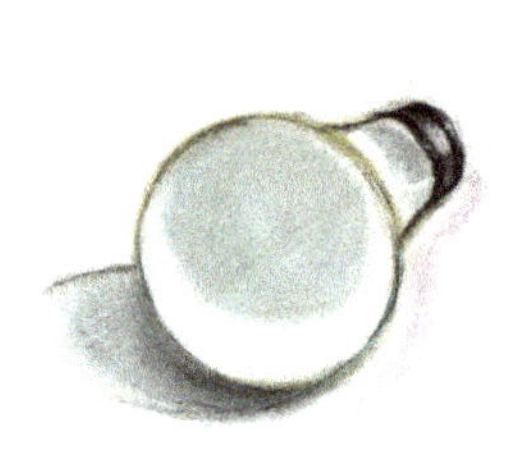

Begin identifying the general areas of color and shadow using a blueish gray. Smudge to create an even tone.

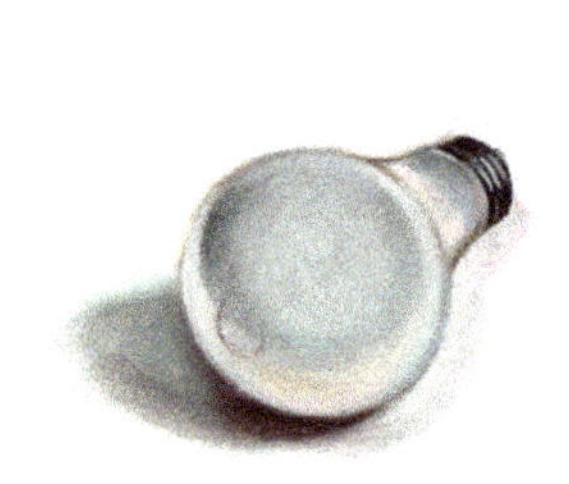

Continue to work generally with warm and cool grays to idenfiy areas of highlight and shadow. Remember to smudge in the shape of the bulb.

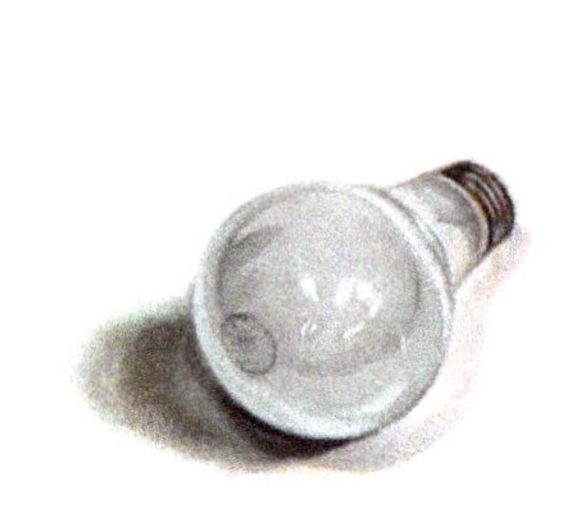

Make sure to use a full range of cool blueish grays to warm pinkish grays to realize the volume of the bulb. As you finish, smudge less and less.

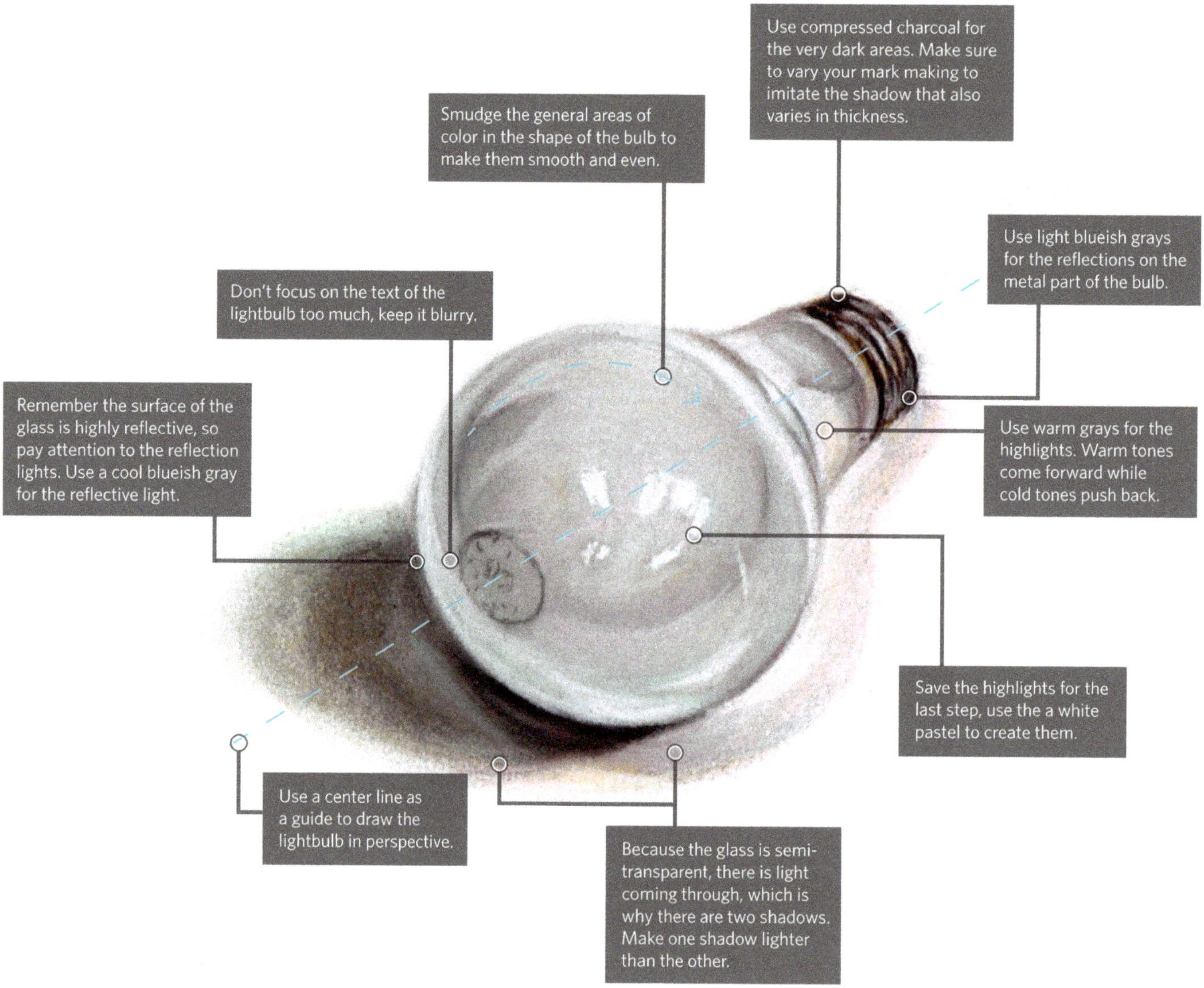

Use compressed charcoal for the very dark areas. Make sure to vary your mark making to imitate the shadow that also varies in thickness.

Smudge the general areas of color in the shape of the bulb to make them smooth and even.

Use light blueish grays for the reflections on the metal part of the bulb.

Don't focus on the text of the lightbulb too much, keep it blurry.

Remember the surface of the glass is highly reflective, so pay attention to the reflection lights. Use a cool blueish gray for the reflective light.

Use warm grays for the highlights. Warm tones come forward while cold tones push back.

Save the highlights for the last step, use the a white pastel to create them.

Use a center line as a guide to draw the lightbulb in perspective.

Because the glass is semi-transparent, there is light coming through, which is why there are two shadows. Make one shadow lighter than the other.

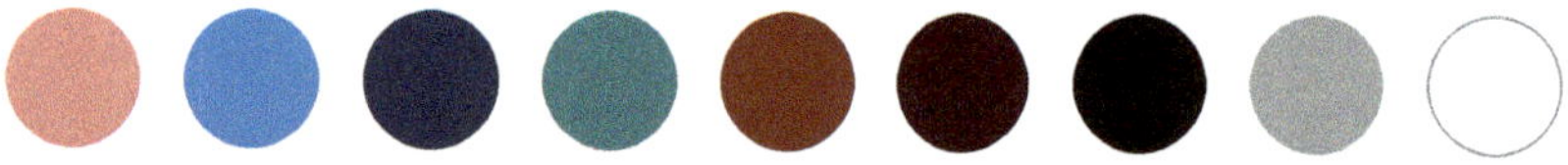

light pink, cerulean blue, prussian blue, turquoise blue, burnt sienna, burnt umber, charcoal, gray, white

Now try drawing the light bulb yourself.

Now that you have practiced how to draw a lightbulb in pastel following a step-by-step tutorial, use the page on the right to try and draw from life. You can draw from the picture below or set up your own still life and try different variations of still life compositions.

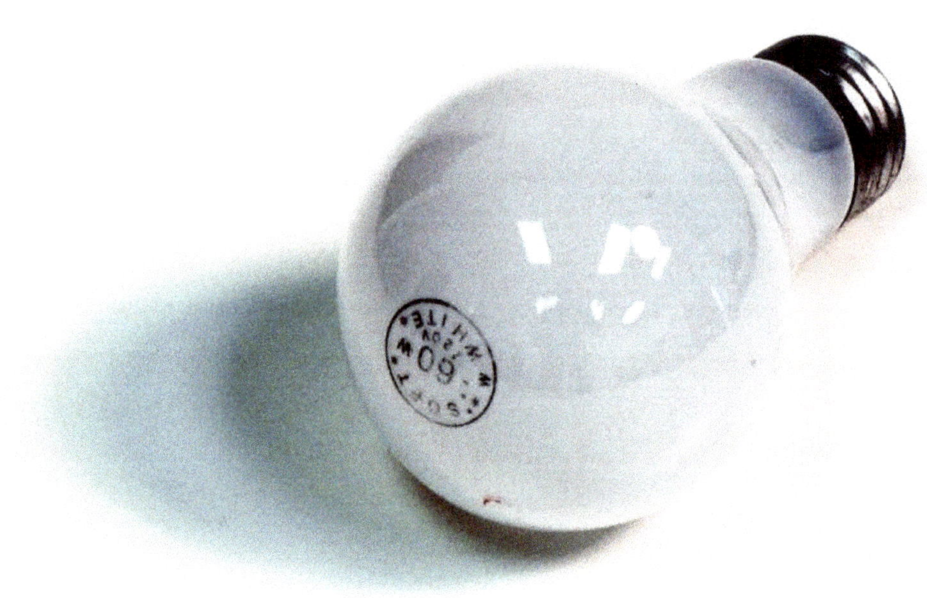

Now try drawing the light bulb using the reference picture without any grid lines.

METAL PIPE IN CHARCOAL: TIPS

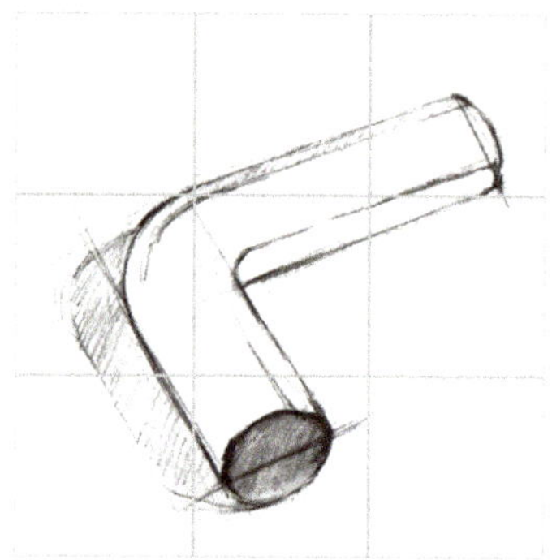

Using vine charcoal, sketch the general general shape of the pipe. Use straight lines as guides.

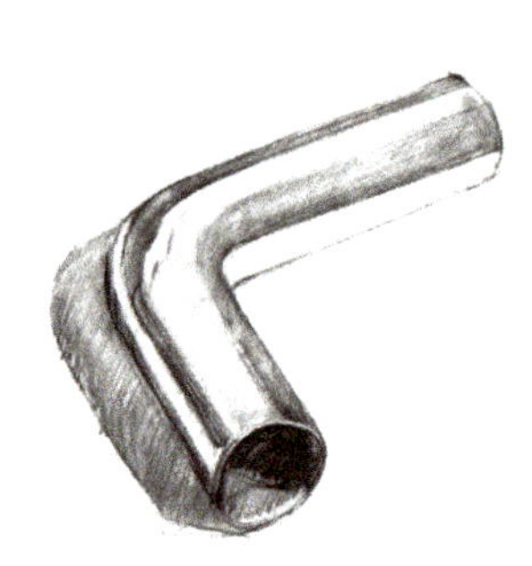

Identify the direction of the light source and shade in the general areas of shadow using vine charcoal to first create a generall sense of volume.

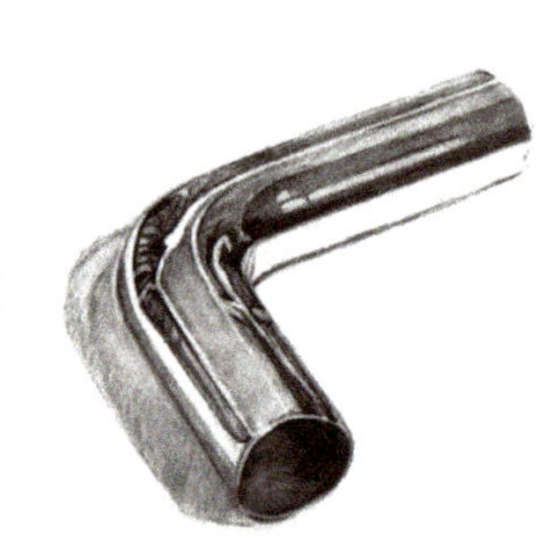

Continue to identify the darks, lights, and middle tones using a combination of vine and compressed charcoal. Generally identify the reflections, save the small details for the last part.

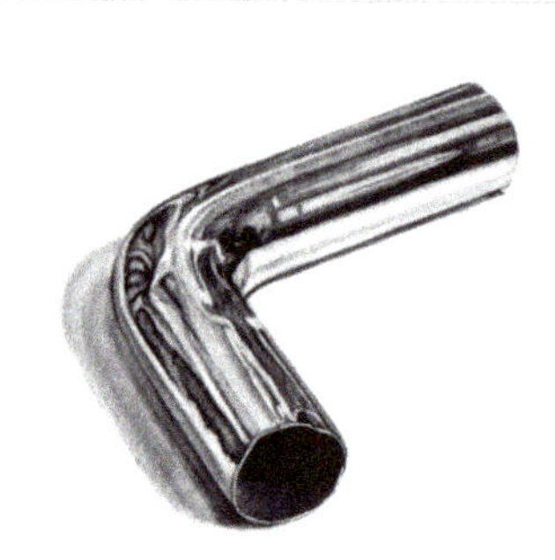

Make sure to use the entire range of tones to fully develop your drawing. Only on the last step define the small details.

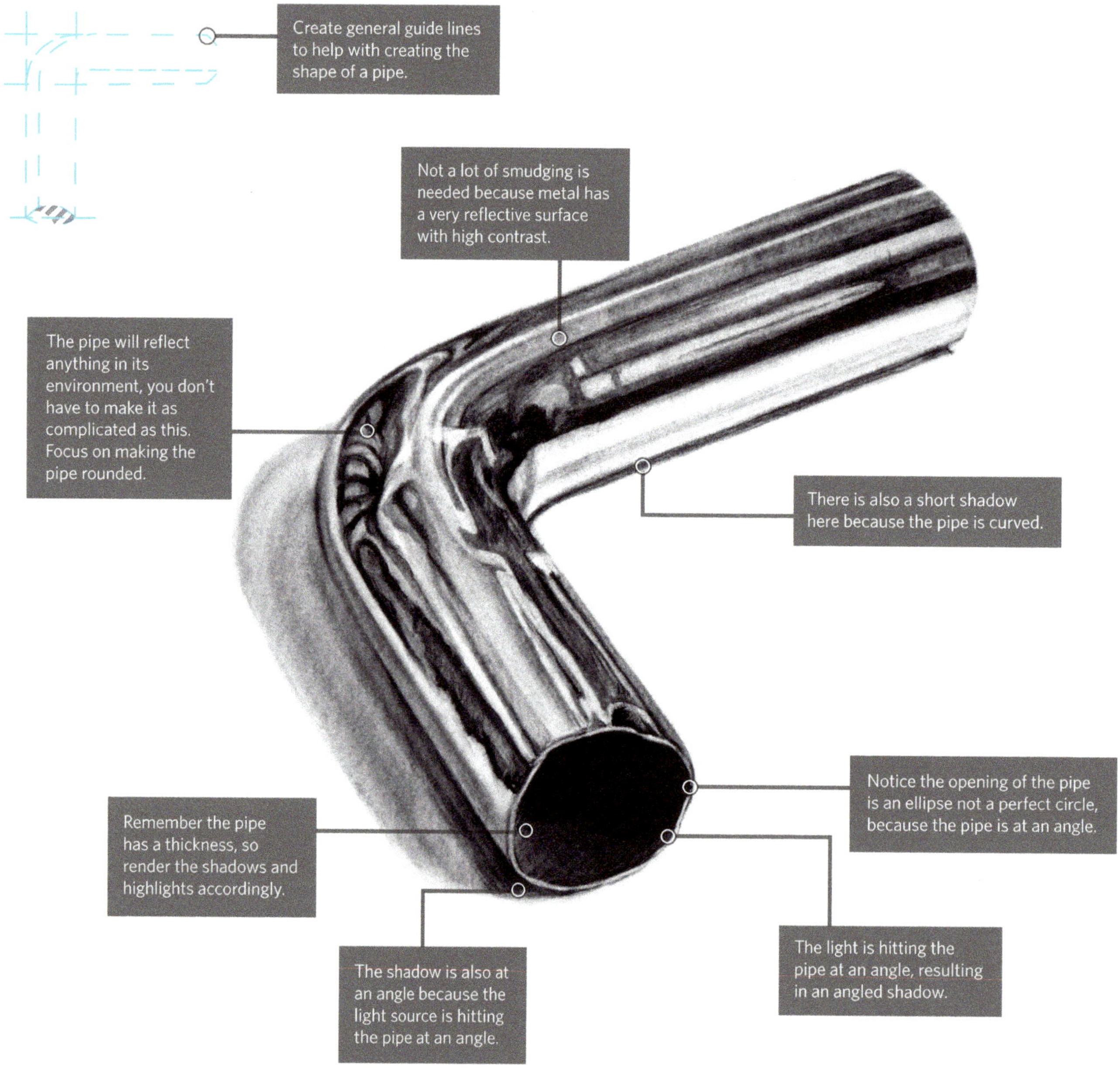

Create general guide lines to help with creating the shape of a pipe.

Not a lot of smudging is needed because metal has a very reflective surface with high contrast.

The pipe will reflect anything in its environment, you don't have to make it as complicated as this. Focus on making the pipe rounded.

There is also a short shadow here because the pipe is curved.

Notice the opening of the pipe is an ellipse not a perfect circle, because the pipe is at an angle.

Remember the pipe has a thickness, so render the shadows and highlights accordingly.

The shadow is also at an angle because the light source is hitting the pipe at an angle.

The light is hitting the pipe at an angle, resulting in an angled shadow.

Now try drawing the pipe yourself.

Now that you have practiced how to draw a metal pipe in charcoal following a step-by-step tutorial, use the page on the right to try and draw from life. You can draw from the picture below or set up your own still life and try different variations of still life compositions.

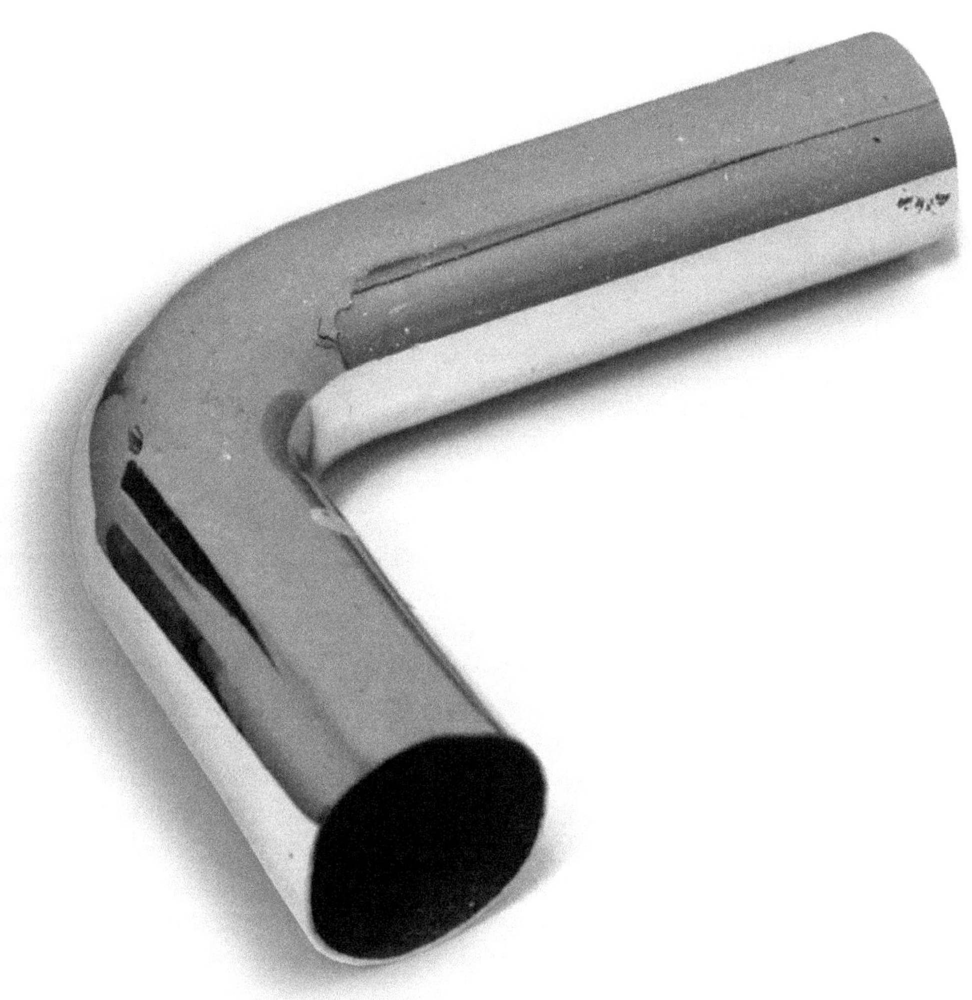

Now try drawing the metal pipe using the reference picture without any grid lines.

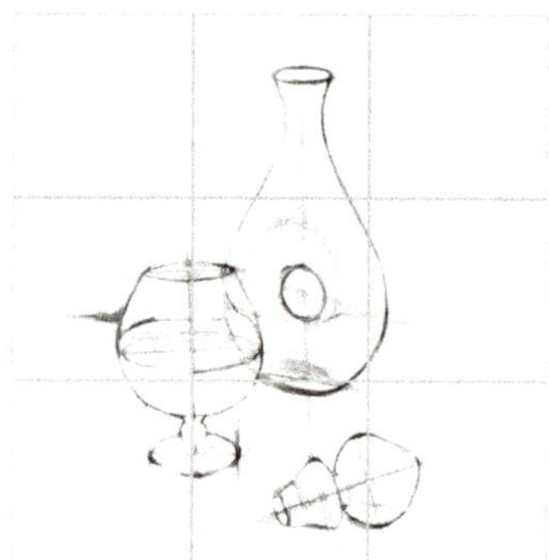

Using vine charcoal, create a series of straight lines to guide you in placing and creating the general shapes of each object.

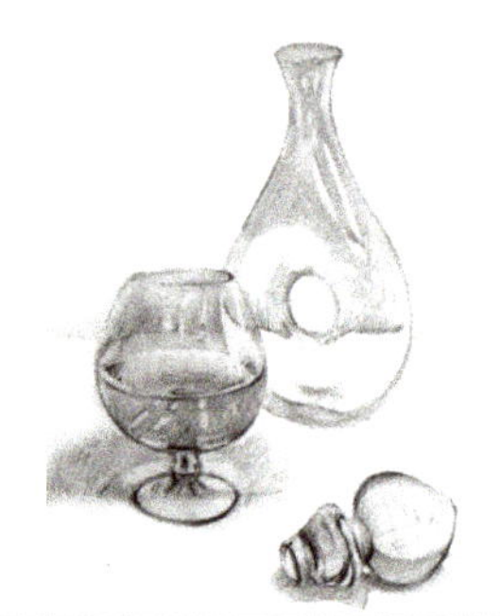

Begin to identify the general areas of shadow using vine charcoal. Pay attention to the volume of each shape and how the light refracts lines and space.

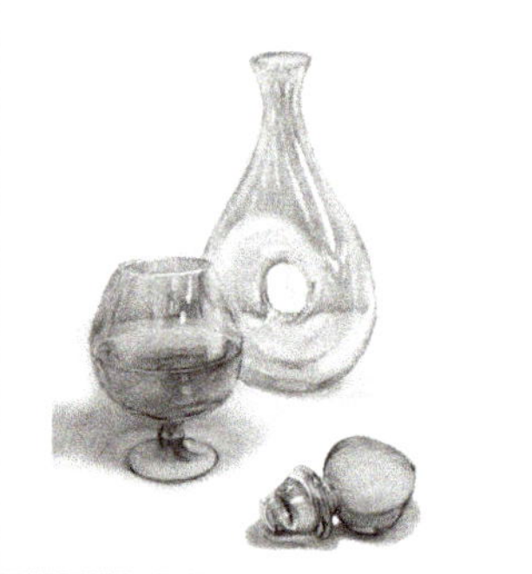

Continue to focus on the general shapes and shadow gradients before identifying the detailed highlights and shadows.

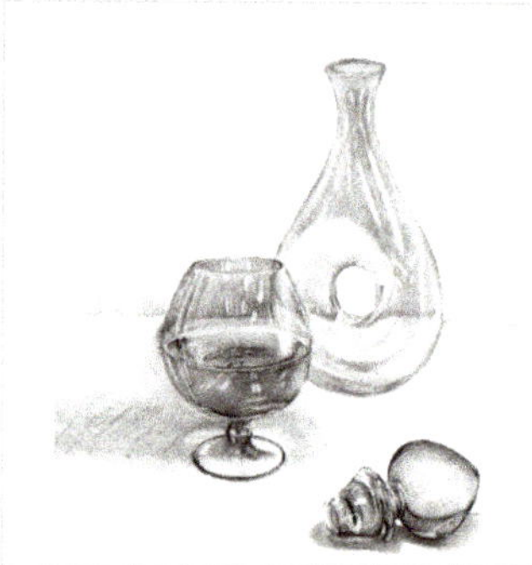

Make sure to use the entire range of tones to fully develop your drawing. Only on the last step define the small details.

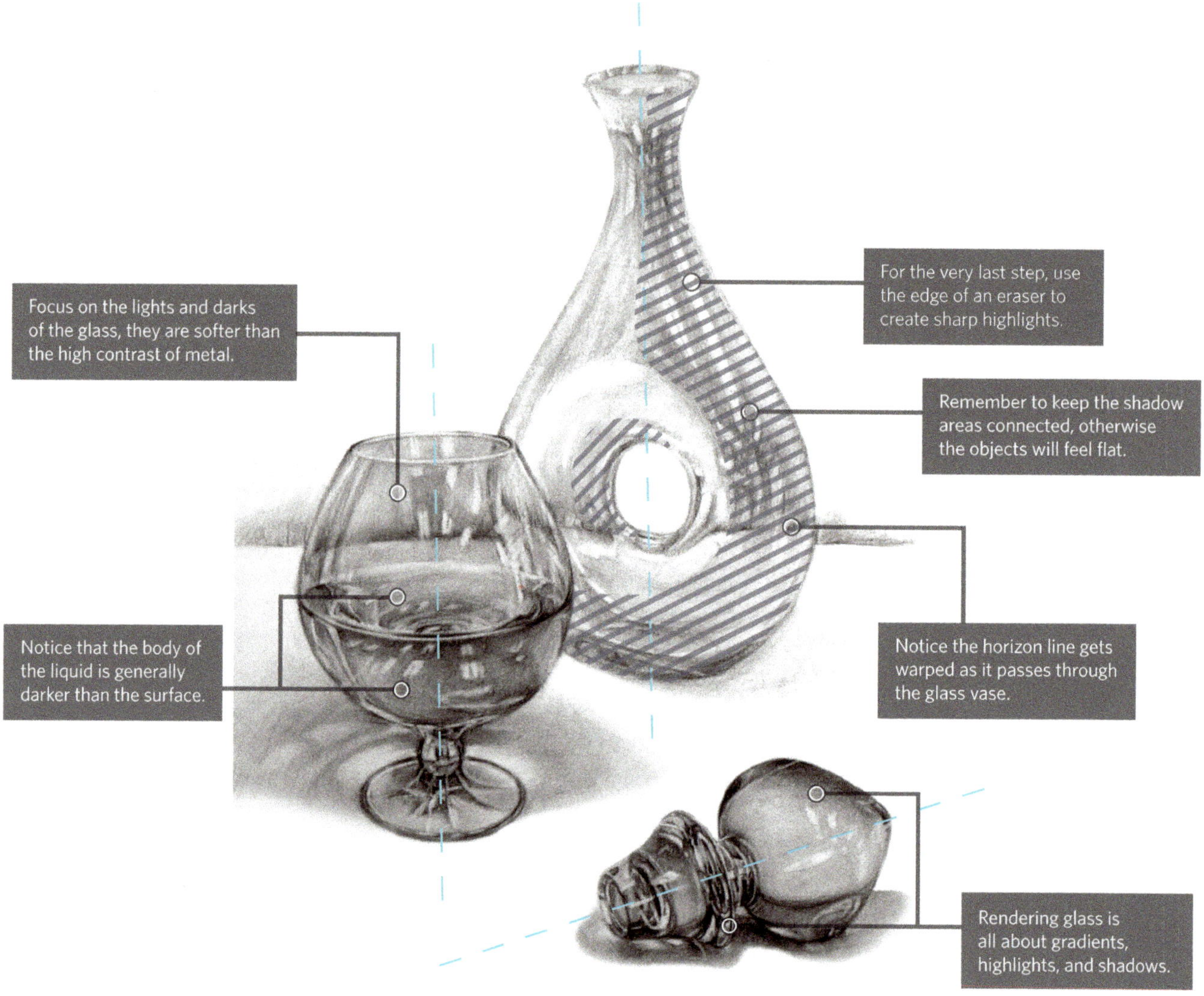

For the very last step, use the edge of an eraser to create sharp highlights.

Focus on the lights and darks of the glass, they are softer than the high contrast of metal.

Remember to keep the shadow areas connected, otherwise the objects will feel flat.

Notice that the body of the liquid is generally darker than the surface.

Notice the horizon line gets warped as it passes through the glass vase.

Rendering glass is all about gradients, highlights, and shadows.

Now try drawing the clear glass objects yourself.

Now that you have practiced how to draw a composition of clear objects in charcoal following a step-by-step tutorial, use the page on the right to try and draw from life. You can draw from the picture below or set up your own still life and try different variations of still life compositions.

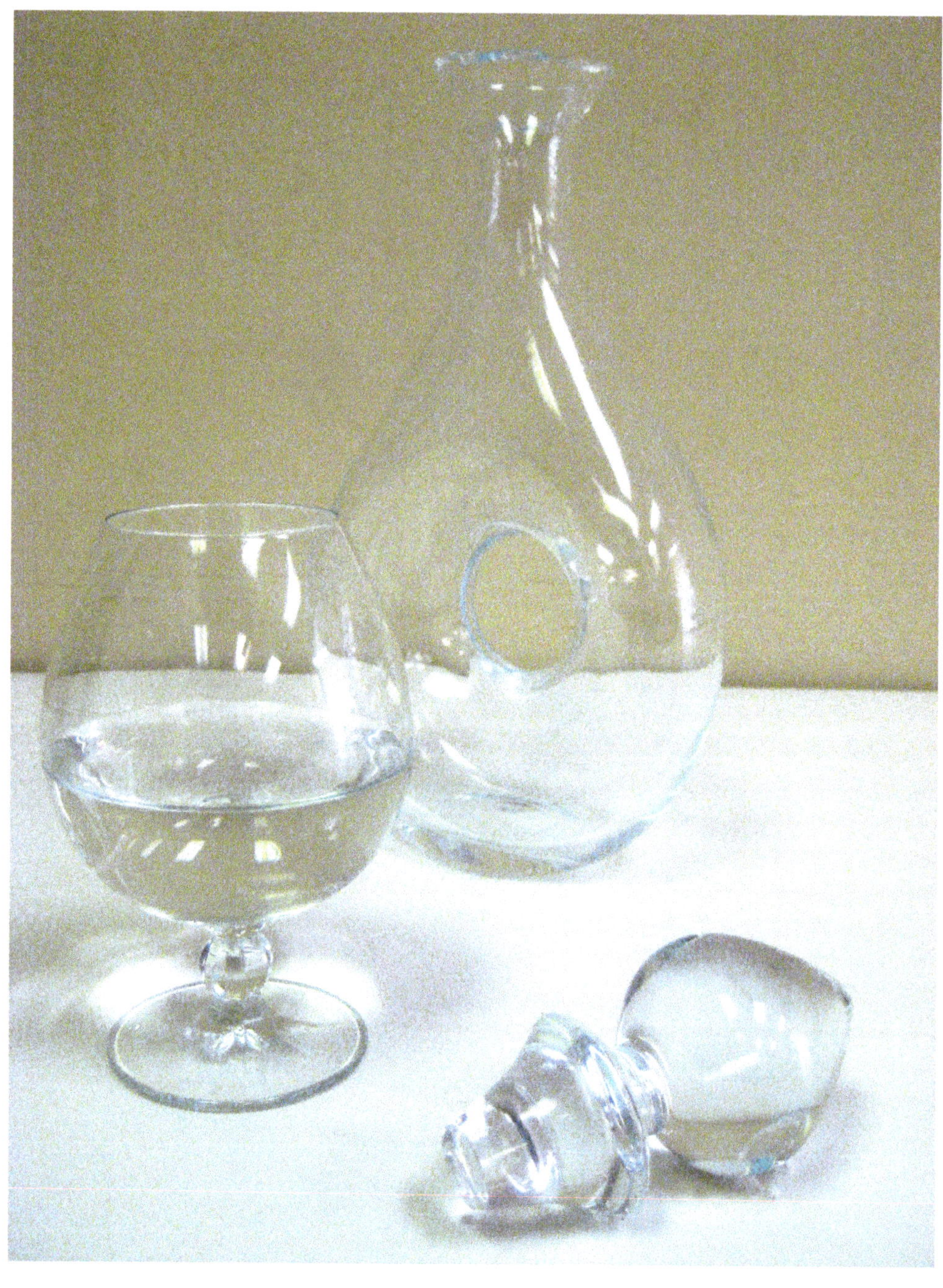

Now try drawing the clear objects using the reference picture without any grid lines.

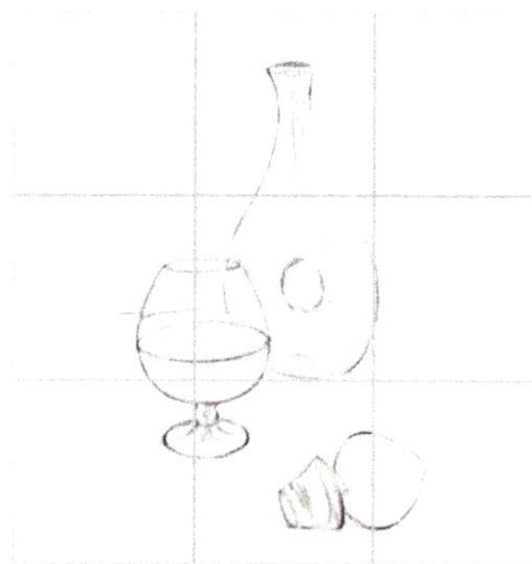

Use vine charcoal to generally outline the composition and shape of each object.

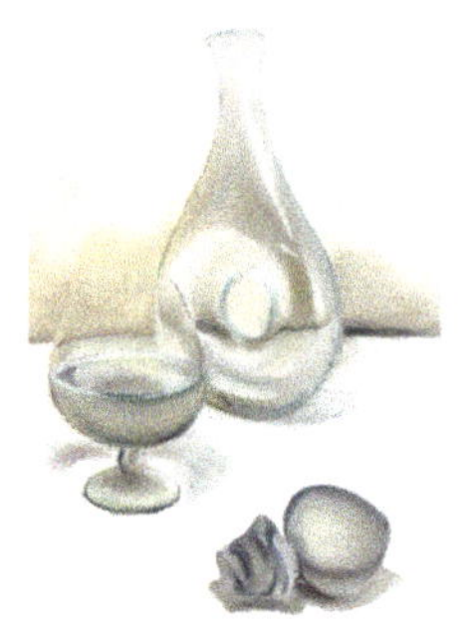

Block in the general areas of light and shadow using an off-white and light blue pastels.

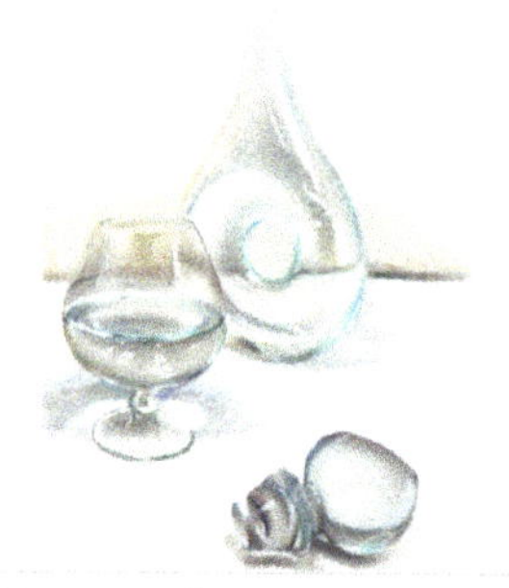

Continue to refine your shading and begin to add in more whites for a more glass-like illusion.

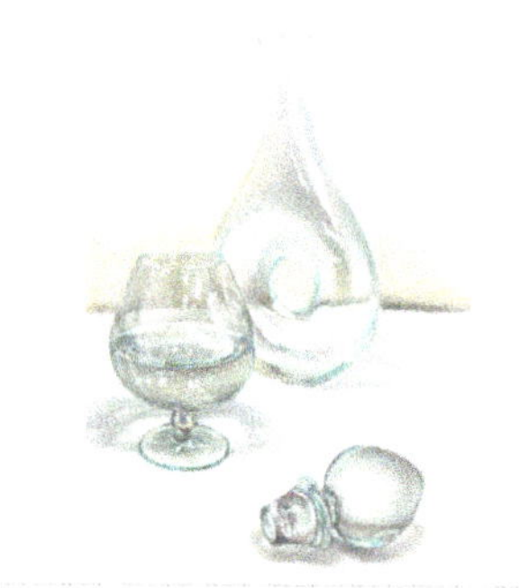

Keep refining your shading and pay attention to the soft gradients being created. Save the detailed highlights and reflections for the very end.

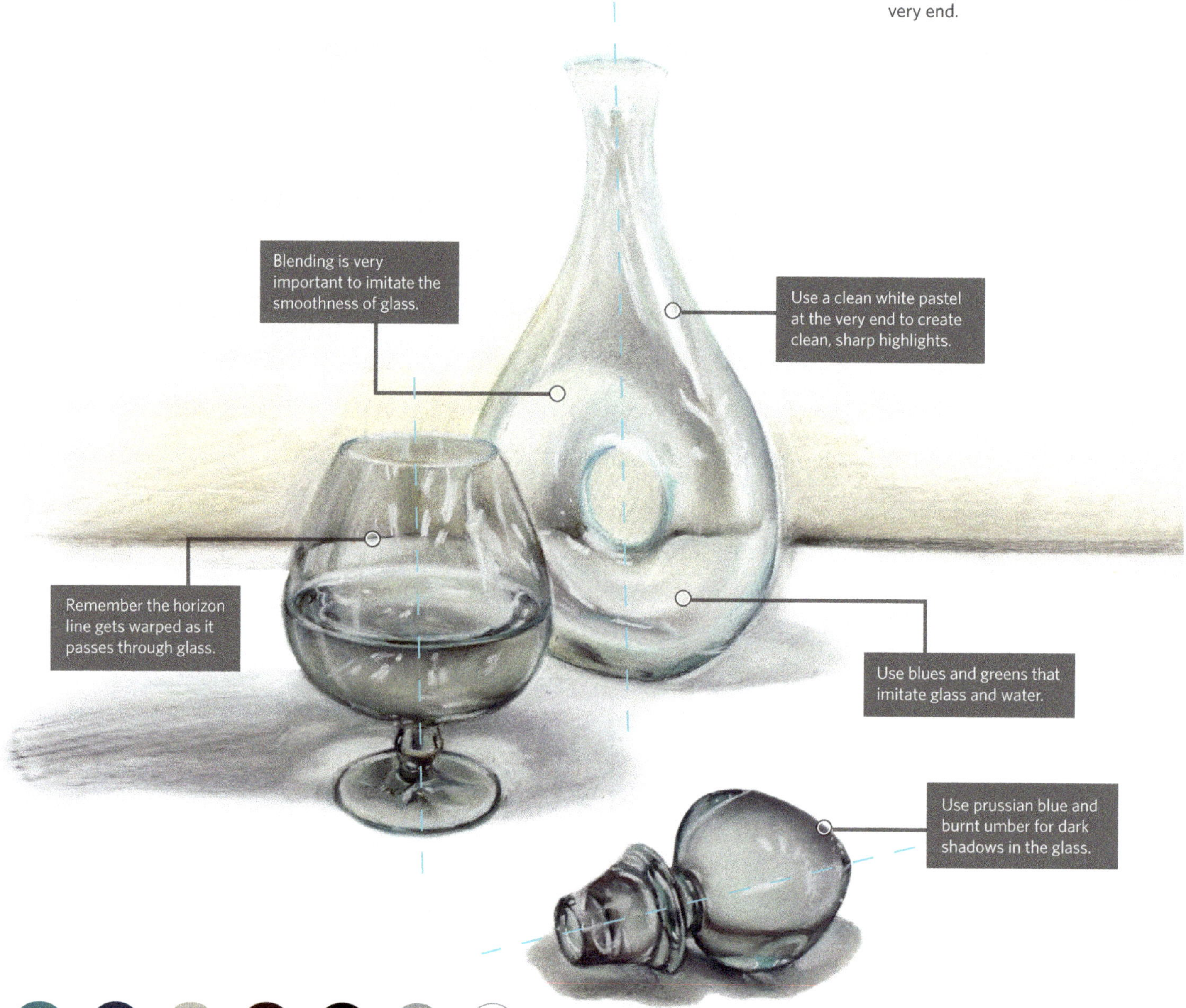

Blending is very important to imitate the smoothness of glass.

Use a clean white pastel at the very end to create clean, sharp highlights.

Remember the horizon line gets warped as it passes through glass.

Use blues and greens that imitate glass and water.

Use prussian blue and burnt umber for dark shadows in the glass.

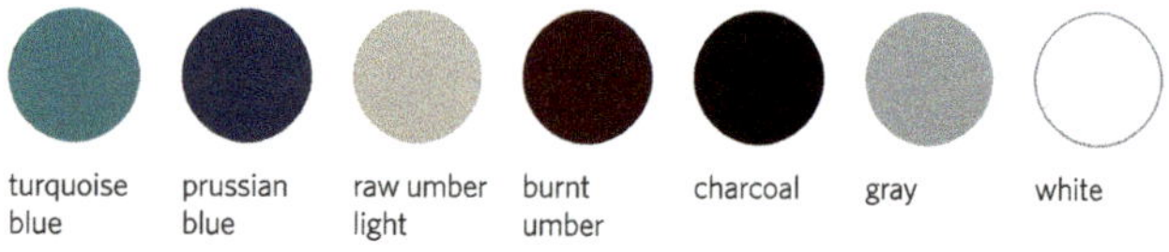

turquoise blue · prussian blue · raw umber light · burnt umber · charcoal · gray · white

Now try drawing the clear glass objects yourself.

Now that you have practiced how to draw a composition of clear objects in pastel following a step-by-step tutorial, use the page on the right to try and draw from life. You can draw from the picture below or set up your own still life and try different variations of still life compositions.

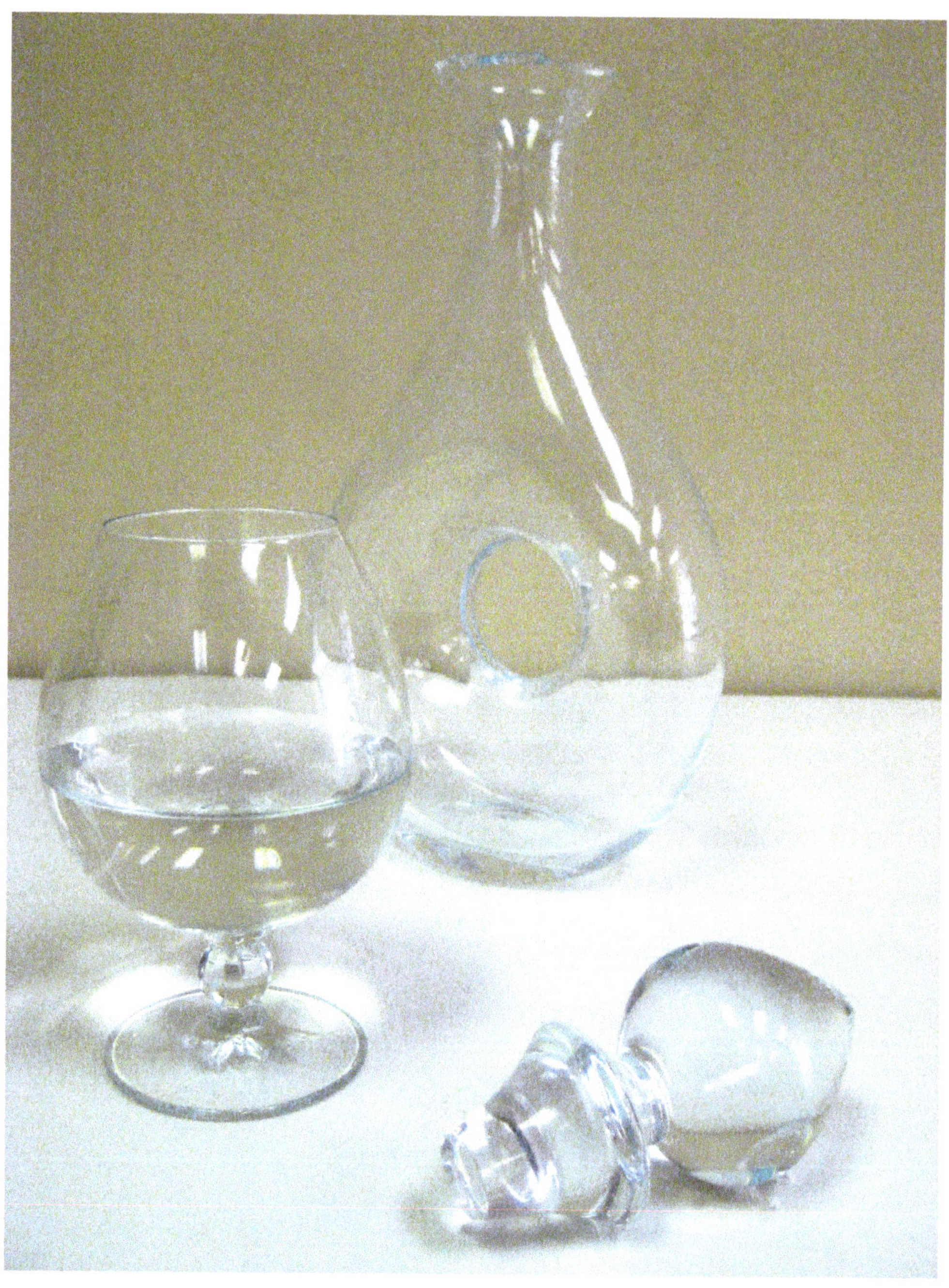

Now try drawing the clear objects using the reference picture without any grid lines.

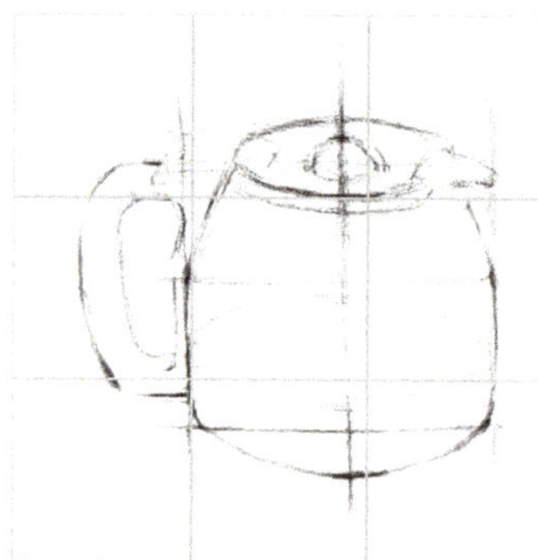

Using vine charcoal, generally sketch out the shape of the coffee pot. Also use guidelines to help you create the shape.

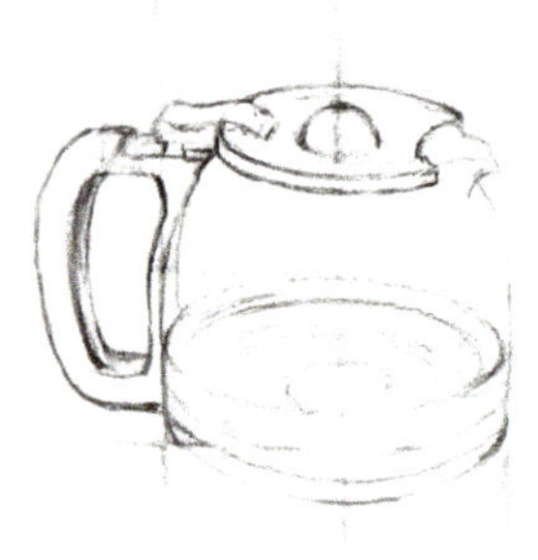

Refine your lines and the details of the coffee pot using vine charcoal.

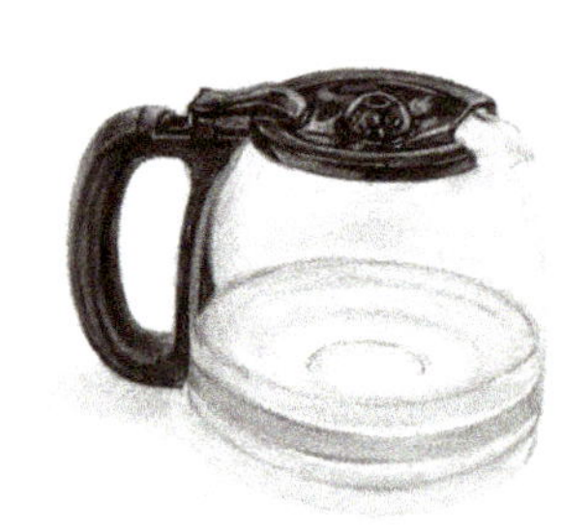

Begin incorporating compressed charcoal for the lid and handle for shading in general dark areas. Remember to work from general to detailed.

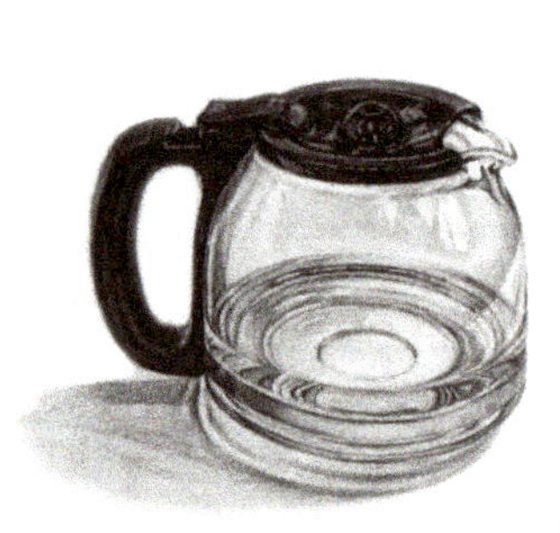

Make sure to use the whole range of tones when rendering the coffee pot. Use your practice with clear objects and metal to render the water and glass of the coffee pot.

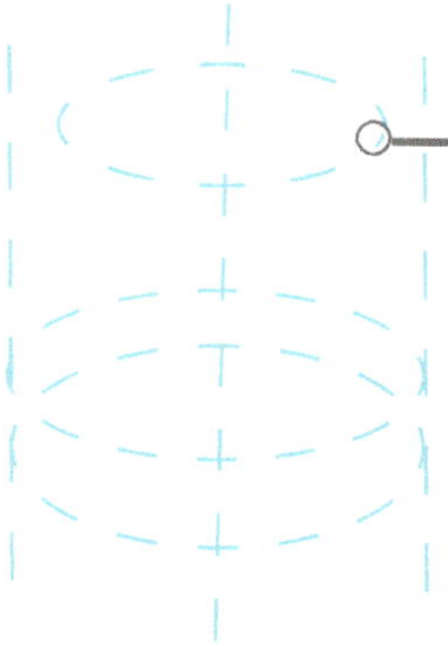

The coffee pot is made up of three elipses. The elipses get wider towards the bottom because the pot is at a slight birds eye view.

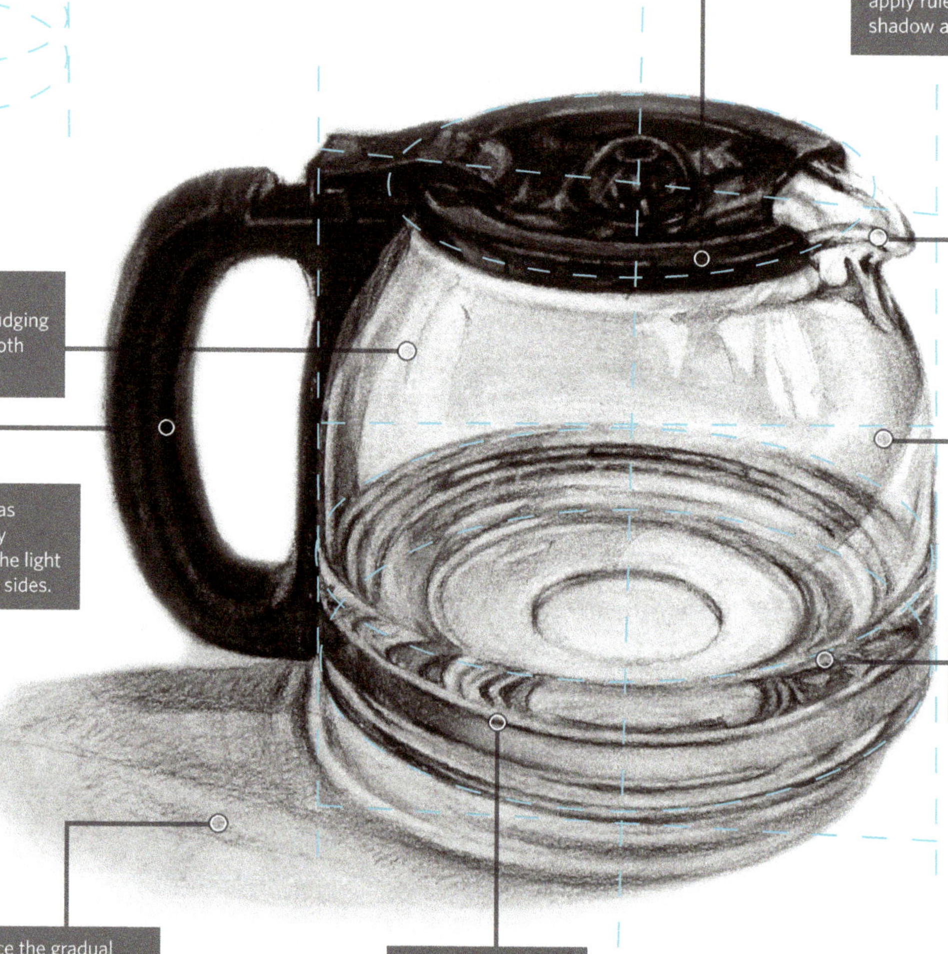

The lid of the pot has a thickness, remember to apply rules of light and shadow accordingly.

Pay attention to the thickness of the spout.

Start by working generally and smudging to create the smooth gradients of glass.

To create the curved surface shadow, lightly shade with vine charcoal then smudge.

The handle also has a thickness, so pay attention to how the light falls on each of its sides.

Remember there is water in the pot, so focus on how the light and reflections react to water.

Notice the gradual change of the shadow from dark to light.

Pay attention to the variations in line width and intensity.

Now try drawing the clear coffee pot yourself.

Now that you have practiced how to draw a clear coffee pot in charcoal following a step-by-step tutorial, use the page on the right to try and draw from life. You can draw from the picture below or set up your own still life and try different variations of still life compositions.

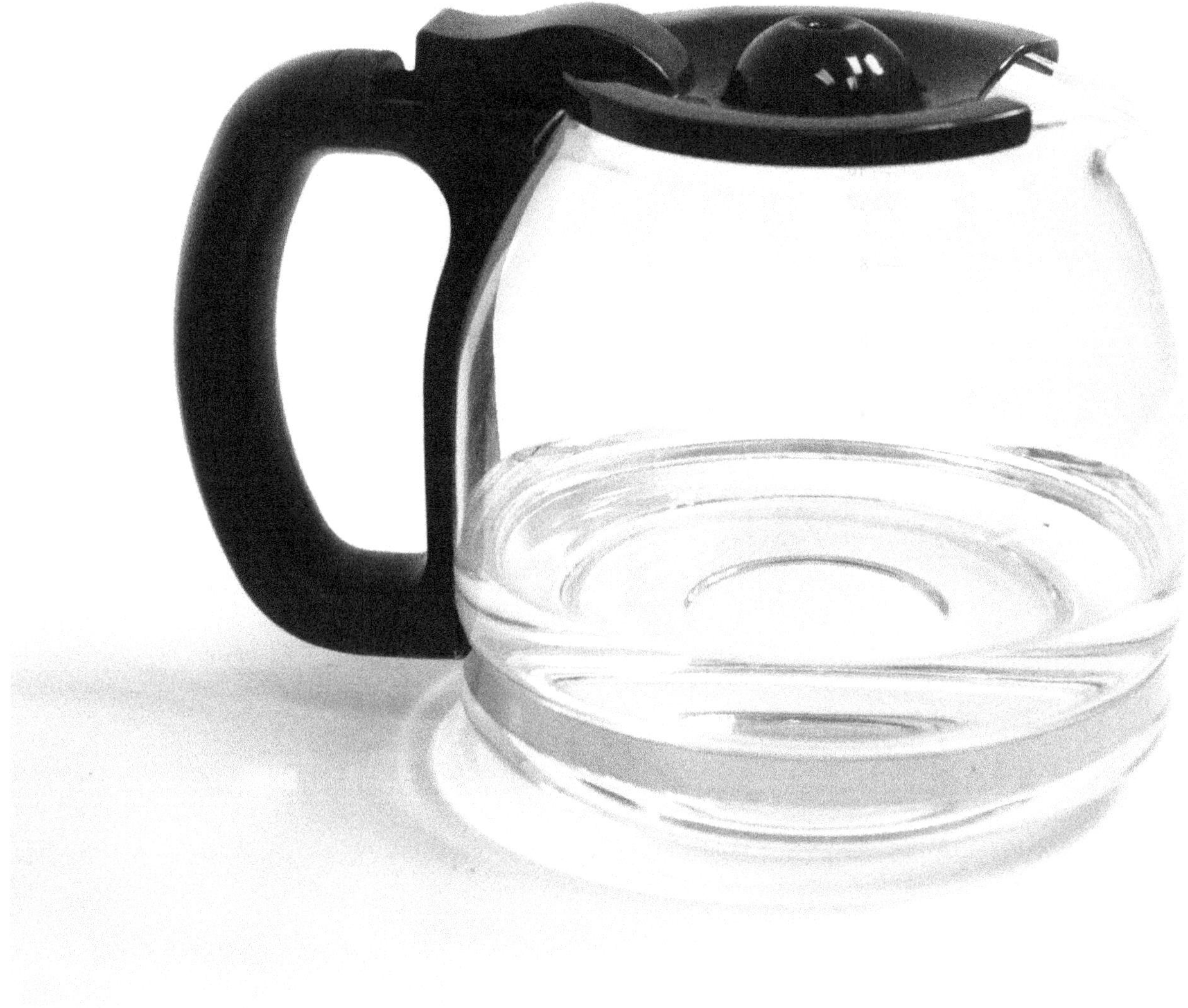

Now try drawing the clear coffee pot using the reference picture without any grid lines.

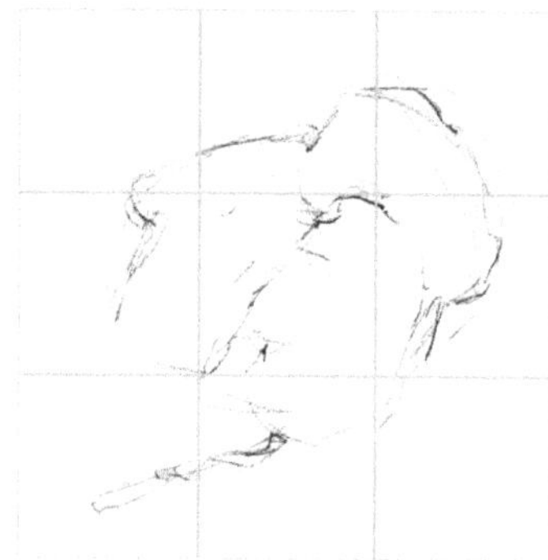

Using vine charcoal, sketch the general shape of the fur hat.

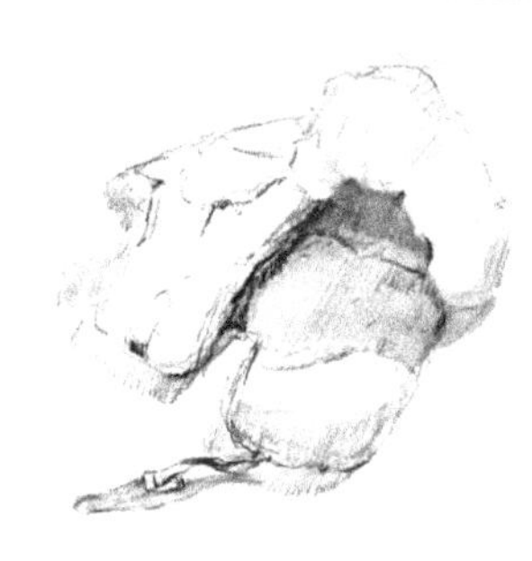

Refine the shape and lightly add in general areas of shadow.

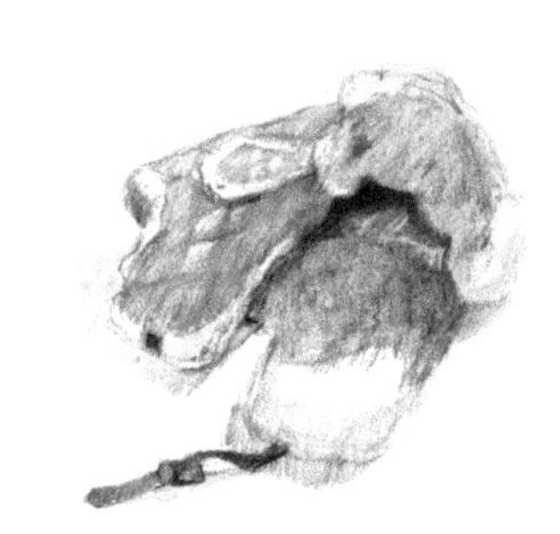

Continue to define general areas of dark and light tones as well as shadows and textures.

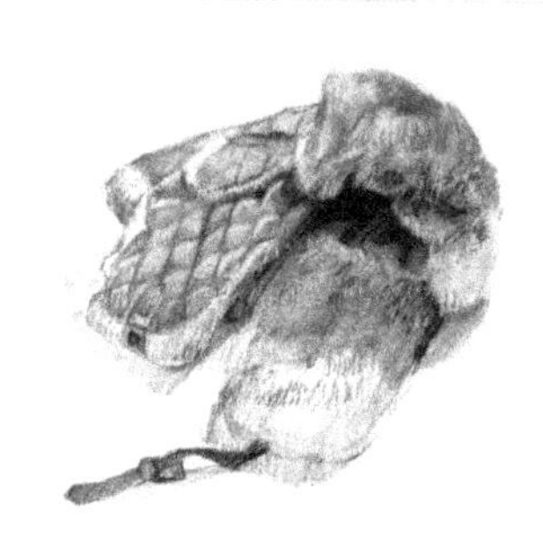

Make sure to use the whole range of tones when rendering the hat. Leave the details of the fur for the very end.

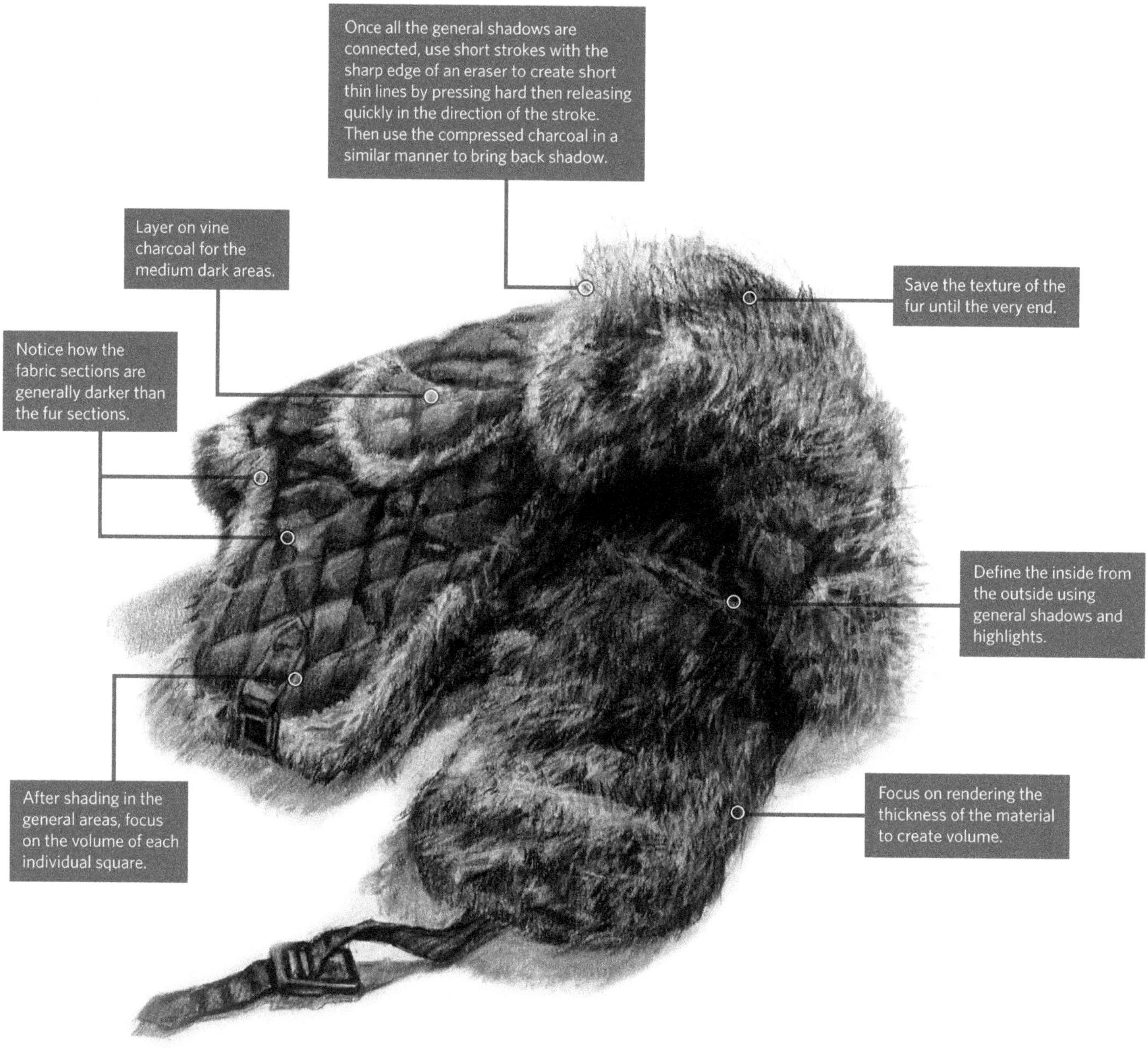

Once all the general shadows are connected, use short strokes with the sharp edge of an eraser to create short thin lines by pressing hard then releasing quickly in the direction of the stroke. Then use the compressed charcoal in a similar manner to bring back shadow.

Layer on vine charcoal for the medium dark areas.

Save the texture of the fur until the very end.

Notice how the fabric sections are generally darker than the fur sections.

Define the inside from the outside using general shadows and highlights.

After shading in the general areas, focus on the volume of each individual square.

Focus on rendering the thickness of the material to create volume.

Now try drawing the fur hat yourself.

Now that you have practiced how to draw a fur hat in charcoal following a step-by-step tutorial, use the page on the right to try and draw from life. You can draw from the picture below or set up your own still life and try different variations of still life compositions.

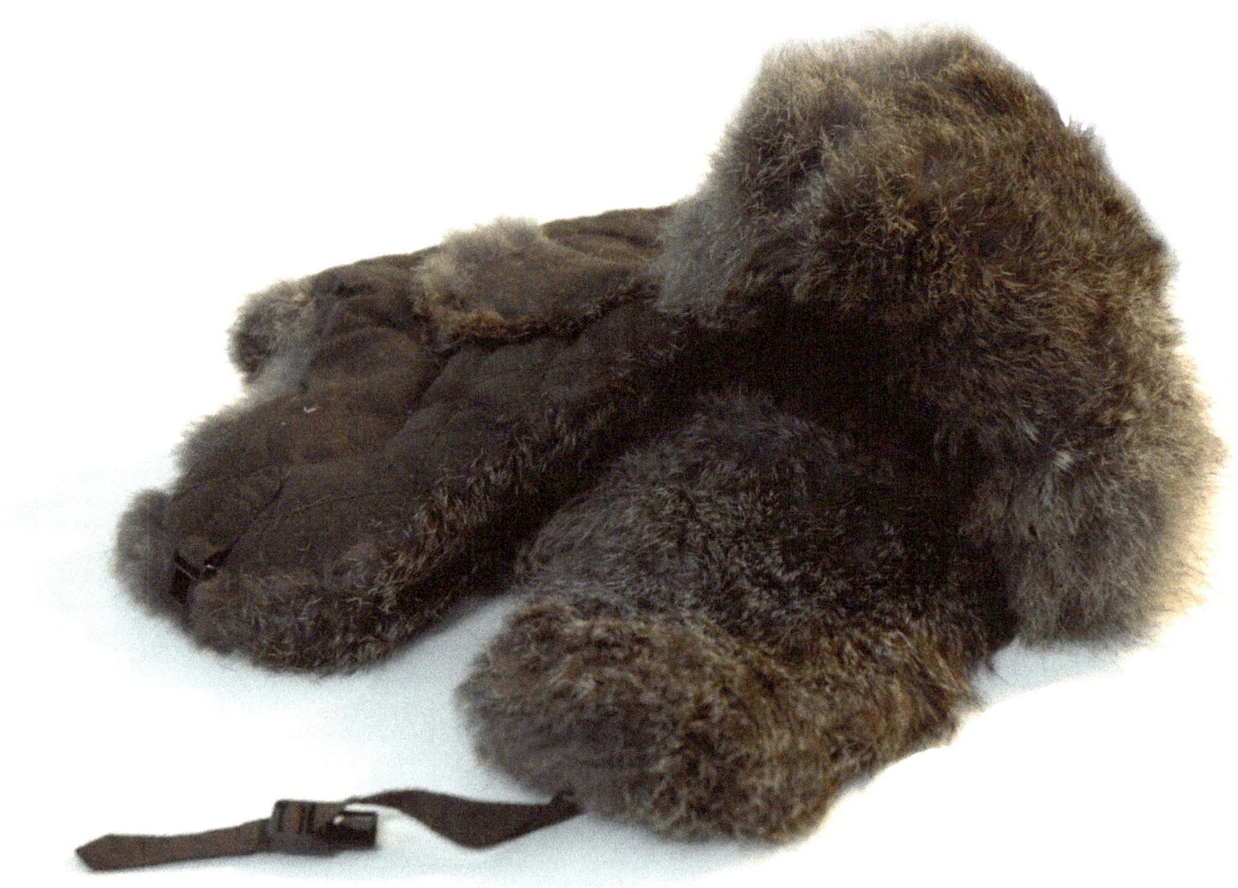

Now try drawing the fur hat using the reference picture without any grid lines.

ABOUT OOGIE HAUS

Oogie Haus is an art foundation unique for its diverse artistic endeavors, including an emphasis in art education, art & design internship opportunities, and volunteer outreach programs. There have been several book publications as well, such as "Art College Admissions," an insightful guideline for students applying to art schools.

Besides being an educational resource, Oogie Haus functions dually as an art gallery and art dealership. Through its research, it seeks to contribute a bigger network for local and international artists simultaneously curating its unique voice in todays art world. For more information please visit www.oogiehaus.com

ABOUT THE AUTHOR

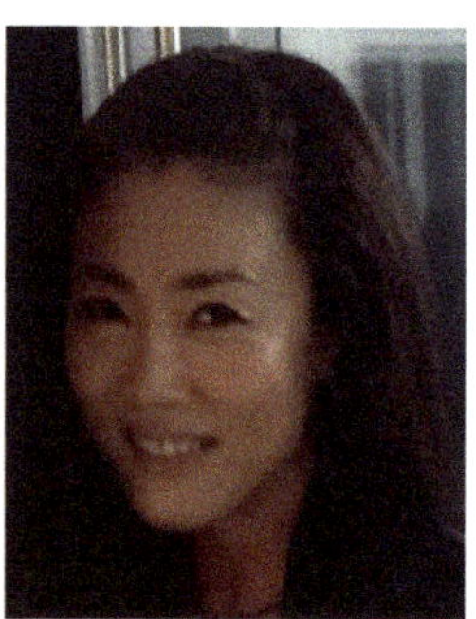

WOOK CHOI is an accomplished art dealer, education columnist, author, art educator, art gallerist, and art portfolio consultant who has guided over a thousand students to college admissions and scholarship success during the course of her 31-year teaching career.
She has received widespread recognition for her teaching methods from Mayor Michael Bloomberg; former First Lady Laura Bush; the New York Commissioner of Education, Richard P. Mills; US Congress member, Jerrold Nadler; the Alliance for Young Artists; YoungArts; and the Marie Walsh Sharpe Foundation. For more information, please visit www.wookchoi.com.

YOU CAN CONTINUE TO DEVELOP YOUR ARTISTIC SKILLS IN DIFFERENT MEDIA!

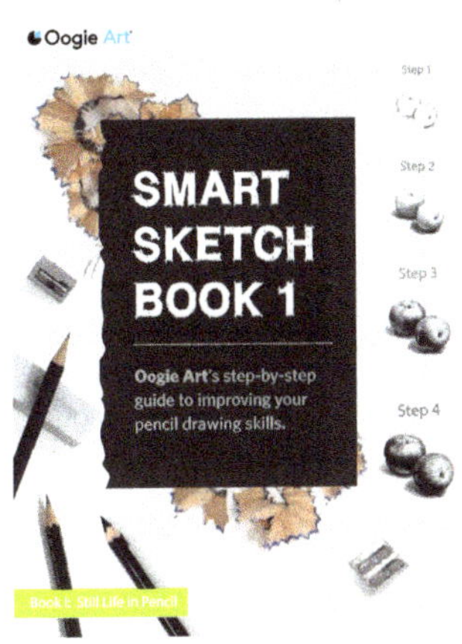

SMART SKETCHBOOK 1:
Still Life in Pencil

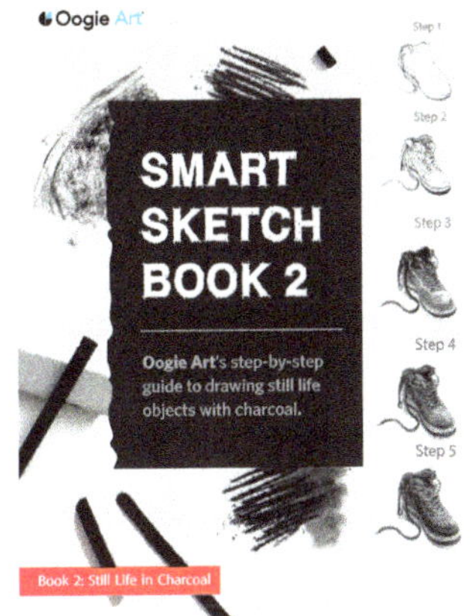

SMART SKETCHBOOK 2:
Still Life in Charcoal

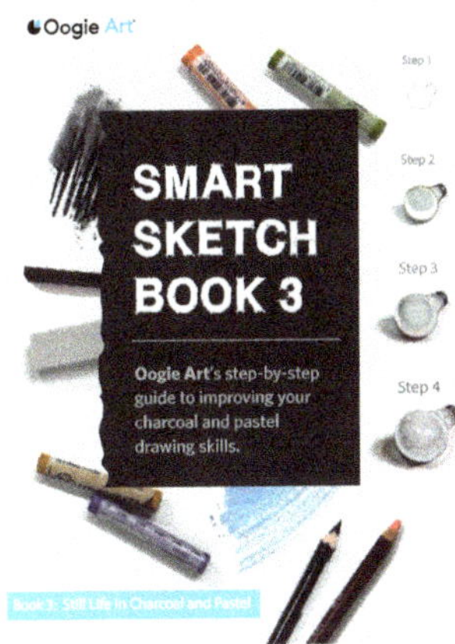

SMART SKETCHBOOK 3:
Still Life in Charcoal and Pastel

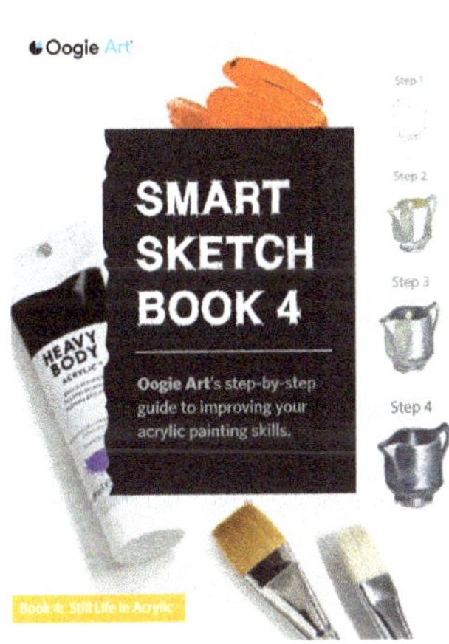

SMART SKETCHBOOK 4:
Still Life in Acrylic

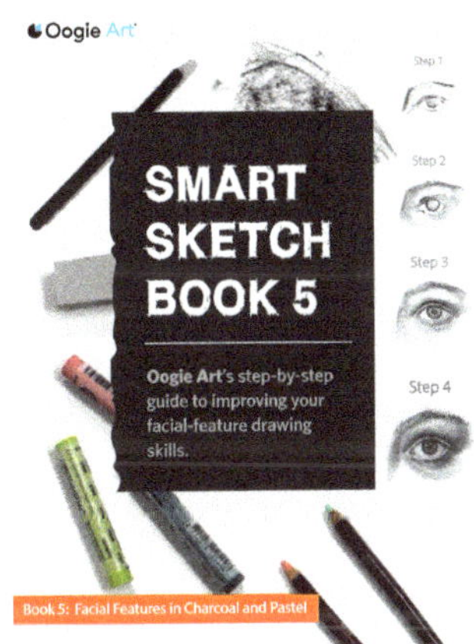

SMART SKETCHBOOK 5:
Facial Features in Charcoal and Pastel

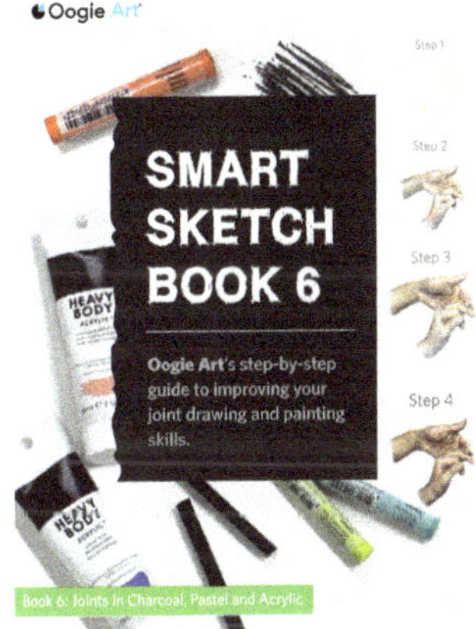

SMART SKETCHBOOK 6:
Joints in Charcoal, Pastel and Acrylic

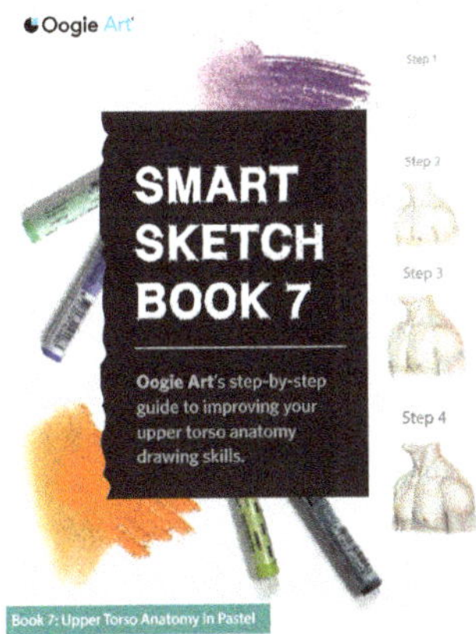

SMART SKETCHBOOK 7:
Upper Torso Anatomy in Pastel

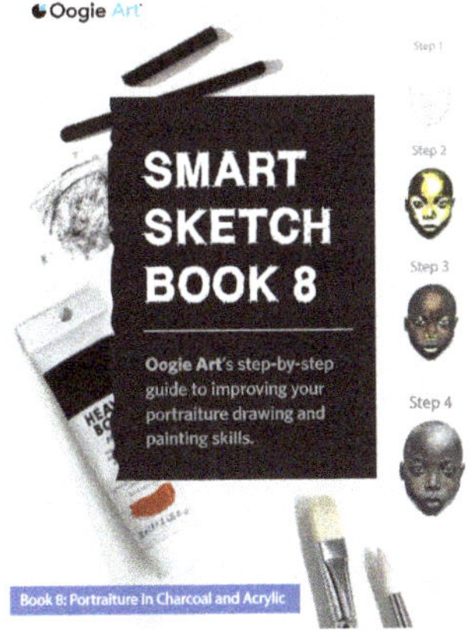

SMART SKETCHBOOK 8:
Portraiture in Charcoal and Acrylic

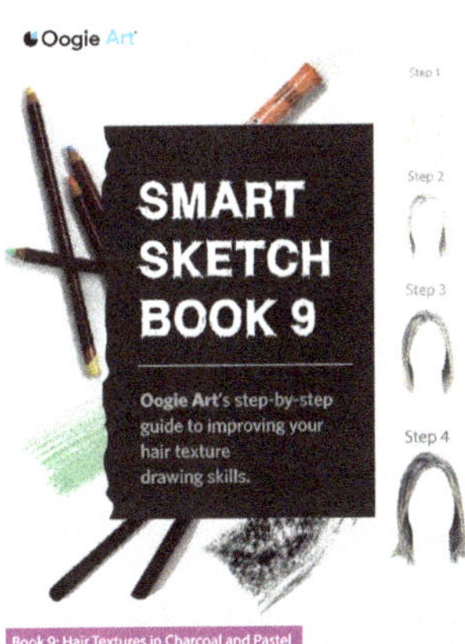

SMART SKETCHBOOK 9:
Hair Textures in Charcoal and Pastel

www.ingramcontent.com/pod-product-compliance
Ingram Content Group UK Ltd.
Pitfield, Milton Keynes, MK11 3LW, UK
UKHW062010290726
14090UKWH00022B/1481